George Eliot

Twayne's English Authors Series

Herbert Sussman, Editor
Northeastern University

TEAS 414

GEORGE ELIOT (1860)
From a drawing in chalks by Samuel Laurence
Reproduced by permission of Blackwood Pillans and Wilson Ltd.

George Eliot

By Elizabeth Deeds Ermarth

University of Maryland Baltimore County

Twayne Publishers • Boston

George Eliot

Elizabeth Deeds Ermarth

Copyright © 1985 by G. K. Hall & Company
All Rights Reserved
Published by Twayne Publishers
A Division of G. K. Hall & Company
70 Lincoln St.
Boston, Massachusetts 02111

Book Production by Lyda E. Kuth
Book Design by Barbara Anderson

Printed on permanent/durable acid-free
paper and bound in the United States of
America.

Library of Congress Cataloging in Publication Data

Ermarth, Elizabeth Deeds, 1939–
  George Eliot.

  (Twayne's English authors series; TEAS 414)
  Bibliography: p. 146
  Includes index.
  1. Eliot, George, 1819–1880—Criticism and interpretation.
I. Title. II. Series.
PR4688.E76 1985   823'.8   85-8603
  ISBN 0-8057-6910-2

For *Martha Kemper Deeds*

Contents

About the Author
Preface
Chronology

Chapter One
Biographical Sketch 1

Chapter Two
Intellectual Mainstream: The Translations and Essays 25

Chapter Three
Common Ground: *Scenes of Clerical Life,*
Adam Bede, The Mill on the Floss 53

Chapter Four
Sympathy: *Romola, Silas Marner, Felix Holt* 90

Chapter Five
Secrecy and Confession: *Middlemarch* and
Daniel Deronda 108

Chapter Six
Conclusion 132

Notes and References 141
Selected Bibliography 146
Index 161

About the Author

Elizabeth Deeds Ermarth is professor of English at the University of Maryland Baltimore County, and is author of various publications on narrative theory and on George Eliot. Her book *Realism and Consensus in the English Novel* (Princeton, 1983), which deals in part with eight English novelists including George Eliot, treats the modern idea of time as it has developed since the Renaissance, and specifies its implications for an entire view of consciousness.

Preface

Among the many extraordinary English novelists who wrote during the eighteenth and nineteenth centuries, George Eliot is one of the greatest. Internationally admired in her own lifetime, she continues today to hold her secure place in the first rank of English artists. Although her high achievement as an artist has been admired by writers as different as Tolstoy and Virginia Woolf, that achievement has not been well represented in the criticism of her writing largely because of deeply rooted misconceptions about the subtle, modern vision that informs her work. As narrative theory and historical criticism have become more sophisticated, the magnitude of her achievement has been increasingly apparent; but this excellent trend in criticism is by no means fully developed and many misconceptions still plague interpretation of her novels. For example, the idea of community in her fiction, the delineation of moral life, the conception of sympathy, all have been badly misconstrued; the influence of her companion, George Henry Lewes, has been overestimated, the influence of Feuerbach incompletely assimilated, and the important, useful translation of Spinoza's *Ethics* all but ignored. This study addresses these and similar problems by treating George Eliot's work as a whole: the translations and essays as well as the novels; the close links in her work between moral and aesthetic value, between thought and reflex, between formal and social convention.

As a novelist, essayist, and translator, George Eliot confronted major psychological, intellectual, and moral problems of the nineteenth century. It is a profoundly suggestive feature of her career that in order to explore those problems fully she turned from essays to fiction, from discursive forms to aesthetic ones. Her clarity about her own ethical and epistemological problems and her grasp of the affective consequences of them make her writing especially interesting and relevant to twentieth-century readers. Her work raises questions about the nature of the mind and about the nature of narrative art in ways no work before hers has done. One of most original features of her work, for example, is the way it demonstrates the relevance of aesthetic perceptions for moral life. She is clear about the fact that she considers life to be art, and this view permits her to consider moral law as a method rather than as a set of conclusions, thereby preserving the imperative value of moral law while she acknowledges the ambiguity of human circumstances. The concern that some critics have had in reconciling her moral rigor with her practical realism is thus misplaced and stems from an incomplete grasp of her work. She is more radical than has been generally presumed in her views of causality, their implications for the treatment of time and character in her books, and their implications for her conceptions of identity and purpose.

One of my purposes is to help formulate a vocabulary that acknowledges the coherence of form and content and does justice to the complexity and elegance of her work. My discussions of her life in chapter 1 and of her translations and essays in chapter 2 locate some important emphases in her work and in her experience, and should help to refocus attention on the innovative nature of her treatment of personal and moral life. Her deliberate departure from centuries of Western philosophical tradition, for example, needs to be much better understood if her aesthetic accomplishment is to be clear and if her readers are ever to have a responsive, appropriate interpretive vocabulary for her work. Chapters 3, 4, and 5 have two emphases each: a subject of central thematic and aesthetic importance; and two or three of her fictional works. Each chapter on the fiction thus focuses on a central issue and on a few works, but each also invokes the other novels, draws on the essays, letters, and translations, and generally suggests extensions of the discussion to her accomplishment at large.

The University of Maryland Baltimore County, the Albin O. Kuhn Library staff, and Jane Gethmann have provided generous support with the manuscript. A version of chapter 4 first appeared in *Nineteenth-Century Fiction;* I am grateful to the editors for permission to reprint.

It has been a special pleasure to write this book: first, because George Eliot is an excellent companion; and next, because the writing has reinforced my belief that scholarly expertise can be addressed to a general audience. In working on George Eliot I continue to appreciate the friendly interest that Gordon S. Haight and Barbara Hardy expressed at an early stage when their encouragement was especially welcome. I would like to thank Elaine Showalter for getting me into this; my field editor, Herbert Sussman, for his civility and patience in the face of epic delay; Robert K. Webb for interested commentary on the whole manuscript; and Thomas Vargish for aiding and abetting my effort from the beginning.

Elizabeth Deeds Ermarth

University of Maryland Baltimore County

Chronology

1819   Mary Ann Evans born 22 November at Arbury Hall Farm; moves to Griff a few months later.

1828   Mrs. Wallington's School; meets Maria Lewis, the principal teacher.

1832   Misses Franklin's School; learning French.

1836   Mother dies, goes home to keep house at Griff for her father.

1838   Undertakes chart of ecclesiastical history.

1840   Learning Italian and German with a tutor; also studying Latin; publishes first creative work, a poem in the *Christian Observer*.

1841   Moves with father to Bird Grove, Foleshill, a location near Coventry; meets Charles Bray and his wife, Caroline Hennell Bray, on 2 November.

1842   Translating bits of Spinoza for Charles Bray, parts of both the *Tractatus theologico-politicus* and the *Ethics*.

1843   Studying Greek.

1844   Begins translating Strauss's *Das Leben Jesu (The Life of Jesus);* studying Hebrew.

1846   Strauss translation published.

1849   Translating Spinoza's *Tractatus* as a calming occupation during her father's last illness; Robert Evans dies in June; Mary Ann travels with Brays to Europe and remains in Geneva for eight months, five of them with the D'Albert Durades.

1851   Reviews Mackay's *Progress of the Intellect* for *Westminster Review;* meets Herbert Spencer.

1852   Meets Bessie Parkes and Barbara Leigh-Smith (later Madame Barbara Bodichon); 1 January, publication of the first issue of *Westminster Review* under her editorship; friendship with Lewes; translating Feuerbach's *Das Wesen des Christentums (The Essence of Christianity)*.

1853   Moves from Chapman's to her own lodgings.

1854   Feuerbach translation published end of June; leaves with George Henry Lewes for Weimar, 20 July; begins translating Spinoza's *Ethics*, 3 November.

1856   Finishes translating Spinoza's *Ethics*, 19 February; begins "The Sad Fortunes of Rev. Amos Barton," 23 September.

1857   *Scenes of Clerical Life* begun in *Maga (Blackwoods Magazine)* under pseudonym George Eliot; 22 October, begins *Adam Bede*.

1858   *Scenes of Clerical Life* published in two volumes by Blackwood.

1859   *Adam Bede* published by Blackwood in three volumes, 1 February; sister Chrissey dies, 15 March; second edition of *Adam Bede* in March and a second impression of this edition in April; begins *The Mill on the Floss;* third edition of *Adam Bede* in June and a second impression in July, a third in August, a fourth in October.

1860   Italian journey with Lewes in March; *Mill on the Floss* published by Blackwood in three volumes in April and runs to a third impression by May; begins *Silas Marner*, 30 September, finishes 10 March 1861.

1861   *Silas Marner* published by Blackwood in April; begins *Romola* in October.

1862   *Romola* begins in *Cornhill Magazine* in July (runs for fourteen monthly installments).

1863   *Romola* published in three volumes by Smith, Elder and Co.; Eliot and Lewes buy the Priory, 21 North Bank, Regent's Park.

1864   Starts with Lewes and F. W. Burton for Italy; studies Spanish.

1865   January holiday in Paris; has begun *Felix Holt, the Radical* by March; excursion in November to Brittany.

1866   *Felix Holt* published by Blackwood in June; starts with Lewes for Holland, Belgium, and Germany; in December travels to Spain.

1867   With Lewes in Germany.

1868   *The Spanish Gypsy* published by Blackwood, 25 May; with Lewes in Germany and Switzerland.

1869   Travels with Lewes to Italy in March; meets John Walter

Cross in Rome, April; begins *Middlemarch* August; Thornton Lewes dies 19 October.

1870   In Germany and Austria with Lewes; experimenting with "Miss Brooke" in December.

1871   Acutely ill for a month; *Middlemarch*, book 1, published by Blackwood in the first of eight monthly parts ending in December 1872, when it was published in three volumes.

1872   Ill in January; in Germany with Lewes, September and October; ill in December.

1873   Holiday in France and Germany from June through August; studies Jewish subjects; Thornton Hunt dies in June.

1874   Lewes reads opening chapters of *Daniel Deronda* in June; holiday with Lewes in France and Belgium in October; two excursions in Wiltshire.

1875   Herbert Lewes (Bertie) dies in Natal.

1876   *Daniel Deronda*, book 1, published by Blackwood, 1 February, in the first of eight monthly parts through September; to France and Switzerland with Lewes, June, July, and August; *Daniel Deronda* published in four volumes in September; purchases the Heights at Witley with Lewes, December.

1878   Lewes very ill in June, worse in October and November, dies 22 December.

1879   Working on Lewes's *Problems of Life and Mind;* John Blackwood dies in October.

1880   Marries John Walter Cross in May; trip to Continent; moves to 4 Cheyne Walk, 3 December; dies 22 December.

Chapter One
Biographical Sketch

When Mary Ann Evans began to write fiction in 1858 at the age of thirty-nine, she chose the pseudonym George Eliot. The choice was partially arbitrary; George was the name of George Henry Lewes, the man she had chosen to live with, and Eliot was "a good, mouth-filling, easily-pronounced word."[1] But the need for a pseudonym and the decision to write fiction were hardly arbitrary. It had taken thirty-nine years of disciplined work for her to arrive at the brink of fame from her point of departure as a child in the rural midland county of Warwickshire, England—the country that her earliest fiction makes memorable. Her father was Robert Evans, an estate agent for Francis Newdigate and a man widely respected for his intelligence, his scrupulous judgment, his physical strength, and his versatility as a carpenter, surveyor, road builder, and land appraiser. When he married Christiana Pearson he already had two children from a former marriage (his first wife had died), a son Robert Jr. (1802) and a daughter Frances or "Fanny" (1805); he and Christiana then had five children. The two youngest died, leaving Christiana or "Chrissey" (1814), Isaac (1816), and Mary Anne, born on 22 November 1819. She was christened "Mary Anne" but she always signed herself Mary Ann or Marian. Later in life she was known to her friends as Marian Lewes, and with one or two intimates she sometimes used a nickname, Pollian or Polly, given to her by a friend when she was in her twenties. She reserved her pseudonym mainly for publishing fiction.

Isaac was Mary Ann's main childhood friend. Robert Jr. and Fanny, with whom she was always on good terms, lived in a neighboring county where they helped their father manage property. Before she was one her father and mother moved from her birthplace, South Farm on the Arbury estate, to a roomy red-brick farmhouse at nearby Griff. With Chrissey at a boarding school two or three miles away, Mary Ann spent her earliest childhood with her beloved brother Isaac, playing in the profuse orchards and gardens at Griff and roaming the meadows nearby; and best of all, riding between her father's knees as he drove his cart about the Arbury estate on business. In these years she developed the affection she always felt for the sight of cultivated fields and the smell of fresh-mown hay. When Isaac went to school near Coventry she joined Chrissey at Miss Lathom's school. There is little coherent documentary explanation for this early separation. As her recent biographer takes note, "five seems to us a tender age to be turned out to boarding school, even three miles from home."[2] There is little evidence to suggest a close relation with her mother, apparently a woman of wit and intelligence, and scarcely any evidence concerning her parents' relationship.

The next step in her education was the first in a perceptible series that took her from the life of a country householder in Warwickshire to the first rank of artists and intellectuals. It was a step that might have seemed to promise quite different results. She was transferred at the age of nine to Mrs. Wallington's Boarding School in Nuneaton, where she developed a strong and long-lasting friendship with the principal governess, a young Irishwoman named Maria Lewis. Miss Lewis was a kind woman with a sense of humor "about everything except religion."[3] Under her influence Mary Ann Evans devoted herself for four years to a diligent study of Scripture and the cultivation of an evangelical earnestness concerning problems of religious doctrine that had never troubled the heads of her churchgoing family. This development gave rise to some very serious letters, much pomposity, and excessive zeal in self-mortification; nevertheless, her early piety should be regarded, not as a culvert by the side of the road into which her energies were deflected, but as the broad avenue for an "urgent spirit" that lacked other encouragements.[4]

Evangelicalism, as she showed in her first fiction, brought to the rural towns of England an "idea of duty, that recognition of something to be lived for beyond the mere satisfaction of self, which is to the moral life what the addition of a great central ganglion is to animal life."[5] During the period just prior to Mary Ann's birth, Evangelicalism and Methodism had a profound influence on English cultural and intellectual life; its impact can hardly be overstated. If it is true that George Eliot's distinction rests partly on the fact that she came to fiction from philosophy, it is also true that she came to philosophy from Evangelicalism. It gave her a reasoned explanation of the nature of things wider reaching than the limited visions of her respectable, intellectually conventional family. Her brother Isaac disliked her studiousness; she later wrote to a friend, "I used to go about like an owl to the great disgust of my brother."[6] Later on, as her mind continued to develop, the rift with her family widened.

Mary Ann Evans continued in close communication with Miss Lewis for a decade, long after she left Mrs. Wallington's school and moved to a new one in Coventry. She arrived at the Misses Franklins' School at the age of thirteen and although her letters to Miss Lewis continue to report a pious frame of mind, it is hard to tell how much this was geared to the tastes of her correspondent. She reports a dislike for novels and theaters and a preference for reading religious history; but the Franklins' school nevertheless opened before her new varieties of interest and accomplishment, and her narrow Evangelicalism gradually dawned into a more flexible and broadly based interest in languages, literature, music, art, history, and mathematics. Here her peers came, not from the immediate neighborhood, but from far beyond it, and some of them had traveled in America and in Europe. The Franklins encouraged wide reading, even of French novels, and she read them along with Milton, Shakespeare, Young, Pope, Cowper, Southey, Byron, Cervantes, Wordsworth, and of course, over and over, the King James Bible with its rich, powerful English. She even wrote poetry herself, and a fragment of fiction.

When her mother died her schooling ended, and in 1836 at the age of sixteen she returned home to be her father's housekeeper. In addition to the considerable work of managing the household and servants, making jams and jellies, and reading Walter Scott's novels aloud to her father, she continued with her studies privately. The loss of companionship must have been painful, however, and she gladly followed up an invitation, made after three or four years, to use the library at Arbury Hall. Here she conceived a chart of ecclesiastical history, showing all the major dates, figures, writings, and schisms from the birth of Christ to the Reformation, a task from which she was fortunately distracted by the publication of a similar chart by someone else. Her proud father gave her tutors in Italian and German when she was twenty-one, something that may have met her felt need for discipline. "I need rigid discipline," she had written at age twenty, "which I have never had yet."[7] Her sustained career as a translator, begun not long after this time, very likely offered the kind of training she had been seeking.

Her early interest in languages suggests more powerfully than any other detail of her life the quality of mind and imagination she brought to her work from the earliest time. To learn a second language is to discover a second system for governing expression and conceptualization. The gain in perspective is powerful. One's native language is no longer *the* language, but *a* language among others, however primary it may be in one's daily affairs. With languages comes the recognition that one's most basic tools of perception are relative in power and importance; at the same time one has access to new power through new tools for perception. George Eliot's ability to understand a wide range of evidence and information from all fields was partly a power she carefully trained by learning and then using at least seven different languages: English, French, German, Italian, Spanish, Latin, and Greek. She speaks with horror in an essay of the hypothetical effort to reduce all languages to one—a sort of Orwellian influence over the very instruments of thought and imagination: "Your language may be a perfect medium of expression to science, but will never express *life,* which is a great deal more than science. With the anomalies and inconveniences of historical language, you will have parted with its music and its passion, with its vital qualities as an expression of individual character, with its subtle capabilities of wit, with everything that gives it power over the imagination. . . ."[8]

After six years at Griff, when she was twenty-two years old, Robert Evans retired and she moved with him to Coventry, five miles away. He did not like his idleness, and one can imagine his daughter's difficulties in living with a powerful personality irritated by his circumstances. Although her social distractions were limited partly by her own seriousness, it was also partly her lack of interest in customary female social usage; she had no conventional social moves to pacify glibness. Soon she had no need of them. She found a new life in Coventry, one that enabled her for the first time to move in the company of peers. She became acquainted through a neighbor with a group of families who were brought together partly through their trade (ribbon manufacturing), but who also shared some quite specific intellectual interests. Their names are central in her letters and in her life, and through them she crossed a crucial threshold to her later vocation.

Coventry

Charles Bray, brother of the Evans's neighbor Mrs. Pears, used the wealth from his manufacturing firm to support his interest in social improvement, but unlike many philanthropists he took the trouble to go into the matter and to inform himself about the social and intellectual questions of his day, even to work them out carefully enough to produce a book of his own, *The Philosophy of Necessity; or, the Law of Consequences as Applicable to Mental, Moral, and Social Science* (1840). Charles's wife, Caroline (or Cara) Hennell, introduced Mary Ann Evans to her sister Sara Hennell and her brother Charles Hennell, both authors. Charles, partly to satisfy his sister Cara's alarm at the freethinking nature of her husband's views, had studied the relation between religious belief and the laws of nature—a subject of crucial importance for the nineteenth century—and had eventually come to agree with Bray that "the true account of the life of Jesus Christ, and of the spread of his religion, would be found to contain no deviation from the known laws of nature,"[9] in short, that the life of Jesus is consistent with historical and natural knowledge. Charles Bray published his views in *An Inquiry into the Origins of Christianity* (1838).

Most influential for Miss Evans, however, were Cara and Sara, women of intelligence and accomplishment; with each of them she began a lifelong friendship and an important correspondence. Sara was, in addition, a writer and an omnivorous reader of books concerning the subjects then percolating not only through her own forward-looking family, but also through the entire English society. The challenges posed by Sir Charles Lyell's *Principles of Geology* (1830), by evolutionary science, and by the Higher Criticism abroad (German historical scholarship on Christianity) all contributed to a current that was fast gathering power and beginning to overwhelm even the powerful forces of evangelical religion. The tension between science and revealed religion was not new. An interest in science, in politics, and in the individual had been gaining momentum since the Renaissance; but in the mid-nineteenth century it produced a crisis of faith that touched all public affairs and personal questions. Mary Ann Evans quickly came into contact with all this activity through the Brays and Hennells, in whose company she began to find her own language for her general knowledge. She soon moved on from church history and theological doctrine to wider, more philosophical issues. The tone of her letters changed, signaling a shift in mental poise that eventually brought her into collision with some of her oldest and dearest friends.

The first confrontation came very soon. Her new beliefs came home to her father when she refused any longer to attend church. Now nearly seventy years old, and never one to look too closely into knotty problems of doctrine and definition, Robert Evans's belief was the customary kind that is portrayed so lovingly and critically in *The*

Mill on the Floss. The rift even threatened permanently to separate them. Deputations were sent, ministers of the church called in to reason with Mary Ann and to recommend tracts; but they all reported sadly that she had already read them and had "gone into the matter." The crisis continued for some weeks, reaching a point where she felt compelled to write a letter acknowledging that she perceived the connections her family seemed to be making between cash and piety, specifically, that in following her conscience she might forfeit her economic support. The breach was eventually healed through the intervention of friends, and Robert Evans consented to let her think what she would if she agreed to attend church regularly. Although she afterwards spoke of this episode with regret for having pained her father, one can imagine what this contest must have cost her. In such circumstances it is evidence of personal courage that she risked so much for the sake of her conscience. The family inflexibility that showed itself so painfully here reappeared with a vengeance in Isaac when it came to the day she decided, twelve years later, to depart dramatically from social convention.

At the Brays she met a variety of people. One was George Combe, the phrenologist, who studied her skull structure and concluded that "she was not fitted to stand alone."[10] He decided this a year or two after the family crisis over churchgoing, and his conclusion seems (on this and other grounds) to justify the contempt of scientists like George Henry Lewes and others for this particular pseudoscience, one of those that developed in the nineteenth century alongside the real thing. But if she met Combe at the Brays, she also met Ralph Waldo Emerson; in fact, she met a constant stream of notable people in the house at Rosehill.

Having studied German with Sara, and read the German biblical criticism, she was well prepared when Rufa Brabant, Charles Hennell's new wife, asked her to take over the translation of David Friedrich Strauss's *Das Leben Jesu* (1835–36). Miss Evans began in 1844 and labored over its fifteen hundred pages for two years. Her translation, *The Life of Jesus*, was published in 1846, with no reference to the translator and with a total payment of twenty pounds. The work was important, but the translating often tedious, and the effort of "dissecting the beautiful story of the crucifixion" made her "Strauss-sick" (*Letters,* 1:206). This oppression—combined with worries about her father's health, and worry of another kind over an offer of marriage from a young picture-restorer whom she hardly knew and finally refused—manifested itself in one of the bouts with headache and low health that always afterwards accompanied severe stress. The Brays took her on excursions to Wales and Scotland for respite. Despite these difficulties, however, considerable though they were, she blossomed under the enabling influence of her new acquaintances. Her eager response to the new interest people took in her, evident in the letters, and her occasional awkwardness in dealing with it, both suggest the results of long self-suppression.

With Strauss off her mind, she resumed her lifelong habit of reading: in this period a varied collection of English, French, and German literature including Lessing, Carlyle, Dickens, Milton, Wordsworth, Thackeray, Goethe, Lamartine, George Sand, and Jean Jacques Rousseau, whose *Confessions* made an especially deep impression. She reviewed books and wrote some early essays for Charles Bray's weekly newspaper, the Coventry *Herald*. In her letters from this time one can sense the diffusive influence of other lives on hers in the different styles she was enabled to develop with different correspondents; especially the slangy, witty letters to her Coventry friend, John Sibree (son of the Rev. John Sibree), where she shows a shrewdness that does not appear in her correspondence with Maria Lewis, who could not have appreciated it.

During this time she nursed her father through his last illness, to his death in late spring 1849. This important person in her life left his grieving daughter barely independent financially, alone, and thirty years old. The Brays took her on a continental tour that was so restorative that she decided to stay on when they came home, and she lived in Switzerland for six months, first in a *pension* and then as a boarder with a painter, M. D'Albert Durade, and his wife. The three became fast friends, and he, years later, the French translator of some of her novels. The letters of this time are a record of unhappiness concerning her general situation in life, but they also show distinct traces of the later novelist, and of a happier experience. She had her own piano, a theater nearby, a cheerful atmosphere, and the company of people who were "wise enough to sense the rare quality of the unprepossessing-looking English lodger."[11]

The *Westminster Review*

When she returned to England she quickly saw that she could not live with any of her family and she took shelter with the Brays. Having decided to try to make a living as a writer, she inquired after lodgings in London. She ended by spending a year and a half with the Brays, who provided a silent, essential function of stabilizing her in this crucial period of her life. Eventually the publisher of Strauss, John Chapman, came down to ask if she would review a recent publication by his assistant editor, R. W. Mackay (*The Progress of the Intellect*), and this began her distinguished career as an essayist and editor. She finally settled, after a troubled beginning, as a lodger at Chapman's in London. His establishment at 142 Strand was an interesting place, both internally and as an intersection for the best minds of her generation. Chapman, intelligent and disorganized, had business affairs more distinguished than lucrative. He was handsome, magnetic, and systematically unfaithful to his wife. His household consisted of his wife, Susanna, their three children, and his mistress, Elisabeth Tilley, who also doubled as the children's governess. The detente between wife and mistress was upset by the introduction of Miss Evans who, though not beautiful, had powers of charm unavailable to Susanna or Elisabeth. Blissfully unaware of all this, Marian (since Switzerland she now mainly signed herself Marian Evans) played Mozart for Chapman in her room, and gave him German lessons there. The combined jealousy of Chapman's wife and mistress ended her first visit unhappily, but the dilemma was eventually worked out with considerable effort by Chapman with Susanna. After a short time Marian was invited back from Rosehill, this time to edit the journal just purchased by Chapman, the *Westminster Review*. Having learned from her first visit, Miss Evans got along so smoothly with the Chapman's thereafter that she was even invited to join them on vacation.

The *Westminster Review* had been founded in 1824 by a group of Benthamite and Utilitarian radicals including the young John Stuart Mill and had had a distinguished early career. Marian Evans inherited it after a period of decline. Her preparation for this work was perfect, and her editor's hand is evident even in articles that she did not write. Though the pay was minimal the benefits were considerable, including personal contact at Chapman's parties with prominent scientists, writers, philosophers, educators, and political and social organizers. Some of the people she could meet at Chapman's weekly parties, for example, were Charles Dickens, Wilkie Collins, F. W. Newman, R. H. Horne, Richard Owen, George Cruickshank, Sir James Clark (the Queen's physician), William Thackeray, Harriet

Martineau, Frederika Bremer, William Cullen Bryant, Horace Greeley, and others including intellectual and political refugees from the continental revolutions of 1848 like Karl Marx and Giuseppe Mazzini. Among these were a few destined for longer and more intimate friendship: Bessie Parkes, the young feminist and great-granddaughter of Joseph Priestly; Barbara Leigh-Smith, later Barbara Bodichon, whose family included members of Parliament and a tradition of supporting unpopular causes like abolition and the new science; Herbert Spencer, one of the great English philosophers; and the interesting, versatile, generous George Henry Lewes.

By the time she was thirty-three, within a year of joining the *Westminster*, she had raised its intellectual level to acknowledged preeminence. Its scope can only be hinted at by a selective list of subjects that included popular science, labor relations, plans for electoral reform, Christian ethics, articles on famous people, prisons, charity, foreign policy, English history, literature, botany, biology, philosophy, and chemistry. John Oxenford published there his pioneer essay on Schopenhauer that, soon translated into German, established the foundation of Schopenhauer's fame. Herbert Spencer first outlined his theories of evolution in four important articles for the *Westminster*. The young William Hale White (later famous as Mark Rutherford) remembers her sitting in her work room at 142 Strand, "with her hair over her shoulders, the easy chair half sideways to the fire, her feet over the arm," reading endless proofs, though always willing to stop and talk with him. "She never reserved herself, but always said what was best in her at the moment, even when no special demand was made upon her. Consequently, she found out what was best in everybody. I have never heard better talk than hers, even when there was nobody to listen but myself and the ordinary members of the Chapman household."[12]

Marian's friendship with Herbert Spencer ripened into a lifelong attachment. He was a foremost English philosopher of this time, by his own and by general estimation. He died a bachelor at eighty-four, although there were persistent rumors of uncertain reliability that he and Marian Evans had thought of marriage. But he had too much self-esteem and too little intensity to be a suitable husband for her. He avoided excitement as a rule, finding, for example, that Swiss scenery was inferior to Scotland's. Nevertheless, Marian Evans found an intellectual equal in the author of the massive theories of evolution, psychology, and sociology (*Principles of Biology*, 1864; *Principles of Psychology*, 1871–72; *Principles of Sociology*, 1876). He was a companion for walks and conversation in which she could refine her own views concerning an extraordinary range of issues, from mathematics and physics to marriage and beauty. They went to concerts together; he wrote for her review. She reported to the Brays in 1852, "My brightest spot next to my love of *old* friends, is the deliciously calm *new* friendship that Herbert Spencer gives me. We see each other every day and have a delightful *camaraderie* in everything" (*Letters*, 2:29). There has been speculation that the platonic nature of his affection caused Marian considerable unhappiness but, if so, she mastered it as usual, and continued his friend to the end of her life.

Her friendship with George Henry Lewes, with whom she consulted about various articles in the course of her work, took a different course. Lewes was an intelligent, witty man of many diverse talents. His excellent education left him in command of French, German, Latin, and Greek and with a foundation for his later career in philosophy and letters. The major work of his life, a multivolume work called *Problems of Life and Mind*, occupied his later years, after he and Marian settled their lives together; but in 1850, a year before he met Marian and at thirty-three years of age, he had worked for a merchant, studied medicine, been an actor, published a biography of Robespierre, a biographical history of philosophy, two novels, and a blank verse tragedy that had been performed in London and elsewhere, and written dozens of periodical articles on an extensive variety of subjects. His animation and versatility made him fascinating company; his conversation was always interesting, and always about science, or philosophy, or art.

His gusto for life, and his unconventionality were among his most amiable qualities, but they had, on their unfortunate side, embroiled him in a marriage from which he could not legally escape. Lewes, at age twenty-three, had married Agnes Jervis, daughter of a member of Parliament and a great beauty. She, like Lewes, had been raised in an atmosphere of liberal ideas, and she had learned languages well enough to earn a living as a translator. After ten years of marriage and four sons (the last died in infancy) Agnes produced a fifth child, but it was Thornton Hunt's not Lewes's. Thornton Hunt, a close associate of Lewes's and the son of a well-known father (Leigh Hunt), was an intimate friend of Agnes and George, and shared with them unconventional ideas about social and sexual relationships, including the view that feeling cannot be enforced by legal or institutional sanctions. When this child appeared, Lewes gave it his name and treated it like his own sons. By an ironic twist, this was tantamount to giving legal sanction to a *ménage à trois* and thus Lewes gave Agnes a lifelong legal hold on him. His generosity in this instance later made it impossible for him to obtain a divorce, and he could not afford the other recourse, divorce by act of Parliament. When Agnes repeated the offense, however, Lewes regarded his marriage as over. Hunt, who fathered ten children by his own wife, produced four by Agnes, but he was slow to support them and left Lewes with a legal responsibility that remained a harassing burden to the end of his life. (It has been suggested that Dickens's Skimpole in *Bleak House* is modeled on Thornton Hunt.) Lewes continued to pay Agnes's bills till his death, after which Marian paid them until her own death two years later.

When Marian met George his marriage had been over for more than a year. She herself was about to make a change in her lodgings. The constraints of living in the Chapman household at 142 Strand had begun to hamper her, especially the lack of privacy, and she moved to private lodgings where her friendship with Lewes soon became warmer and more intimate. They not only shared thoughts and affection, they shared work; when George fell ill for some weeks Marian oversaw his publications as well as her own, always working under deadlines. She was now commuting to Chapman's, where financial affairs were becoming more and more entangled, and by 1854 she had begun translating Feuerbach's *The Essence of Christianity* (*Das Wesen Christentums*, 1841), a work of major intellectual importance in England and Europe. The possibility of living with Lewes had surely presented itself, but so had a thousand difficulties, including George's marriage, and the probable reaction of mid-Victorian English society, even the most liberal. Her friends knew little of Lewes's circumstances and did not especially like him. Furthermore his first affection might cool and leave her doubly estranged, from her society and friends, and from the man she had not married.

She took the step. Telling almost no one except Charles Bray and John Chapman, she embarked with Lewes for Germany where they spent eight months, chiefly in Weimar and Berlin, while the tempest of gossip and rumor blew about London. The Brays and Sara Hennell, after a slight initial turbulence, remained faithful, but there were few others. There was a rash of sympathy for Agnes, who took Lewes's money and continued having Hunt's children. Combe, the phrenologist, again demonstrated his ability to read character by inquiring "whether there is insanity in Miss Evans's family," sanity apparently being gauged by how completely one followed convention. [13] The following letter, from Thomas Woolner, the Pre-Raphaelite sculptor, shows what Marian and Lewes could look forward to back at London in the way of social prejudice: "Blackguard Lewes has bolted with a———and is living in Germany with her. I believe it dangerous to write facts of anyone nowadays so I will not further lift the mantle and display the filthy contaminations of these hideous satyrs and smirking moralists . . . stink pots of humanity" (Letters, 2:175–76). They had cut themselves off from respectable society, though given this instance of respectability the bargain could seem well worth it. Just as she had done when she quit going to church on principles, Marian Evans again cut herself off by acting on conscience. "Light and easily broken ties are what I neither desire theoretically nor could live for practically," she wrote to Cara. "Women who are satisfied with such ties do *not* act as I have done—they obtain what they desire and are still invited to dinner" (Letters, 2:214). The hatred and distortion strained them daily and for months, even at a distance. The letters are full of references to it. George wrote gratefully to Carlyle, expressing his shock at hearing a friendly and affirmative reaction. "One must have been, like me, long misjudged and harshly judged without power of explanation, to understand the feelings which such a letter creates. My heart yearned towards you as I read it. It has given me new courage" (Letters, 2:176). The refusal to be thwarted by convention, the courageous and principled choice, pruned the orchard, cutting away the relationships that, when the crisis came, proved to be merely underbrush, and clearing an area for taller, greater growths. The action was not to be chosen if it could be avoided; but not to be avoided if choice was necessary. This experience and others like it helped to strengthen George Eliot's disgust for automatic piety and her sympathy with struggling, erring human creatures.

Weimar

Victorian London notwithstanding, however, they had a happy and productive time in Germany. When they arrived they met Strauss, whose work she had translated. Strauss, being a major figure in German letters, was well connected, and he gave them a letter of introduction to Gustave Scholl, director of the Art Institute in Weimar and an invaluable friend to George and Marian. This particular connection opened a wide circle of the most fascinating people, including artists and royalty, and the most rewarding of which for the Leweses was the composer Franz Liszt. They both read and worked hard; their serious want of money made such employment necessary. Marian's Feuerbach translation was being published, and she now turned to Spinoza for moral support and to writing essays for cash. She had translated part of Spinoza's *Tractatus Theologicus-politicus* for Charles Bray some years before, and a few passages from the *Ethics*; she now undertook to translate the entire *Ethics* during the next year. Together with Feuerbach, this work has a major place in her intellectual biography and is treated separately in chapter 2. For Chapman she wrote a series of brilliant essays—her first subject was women—that are still important not only as her work but also as part of nineteenth-century intellectual and cultural history, and some as masterpieces of controversial wit. Lewes collected material for the biography of Goethe, the great German poet, upon which he had been working for ten years. They found Berlin less socially congenial than Weimar but more valuable for work. George talked to people who had known Goethe and collected source material while Marian translated German passages for his use. When he finally published his biography it did very well financially, and continued in print; it is still a standard work.

All the while they worked together, and read aloud together books of common interest. This lifelong habit is a clue to the collaboration that benefited the work of each for so many years. One senses always behind the letters and records of business, the joint collaboration of two minds with similar interests and different emphases, each drawing on and contributing to the thinking and reading of the other. Both came to Spinoza and Goethe independently. The passages from Goethe in George's biography were translated by Marian; her written reflections about their later scientific expeditions to Ilfracombe (an English coastal town) appeared in his *Sea Side Studies*. She profited from his knowledge of publishers, ending her pattern of doing work with scarcely any pay, and afterwards her financial transactions with publishers were (necessarily) deliberately negotiated. But each had an independent mind, mature by the time they met. She knew about science quite apart from him, and he about literature quite apart from her. The professional and intellectual influence between them was of the best kind: mutual, continuous, and limited.

Eight months after leaving England and living, as they did ever after, as Mr. and Mrs. Lewes, Marian and George returned to face social opinion and to live (not without cost) in spite of it. The period was emotionally tumultuous. After long companionship in Germany, Marian spent five weeks alone, reading Shakespeare and translating the last two books of Spinoza's *Ethics*, while she waited for George to get a clear confirmation from Agnes in London that she had no intention of returning to him: a possibility that, however remote, must have contributed heavily to the depression and tension that she attempted to walk off along the cliffs at Dover. George, for his part, found that Agnes had gone heavily into debt in his absence and that Hunt was offering no support. He and Marian finally settled in lodgings near London and began a new life. He was thirty-eight and she was thirty-six.

Given their financial distresses, Chapman's offer to Marian of the Belles Lettres Review section of the *Westminster* meant a welcome addition of fifty pounds a year, and for two years she wrote a variety of interesting and important essays for this journal. She had already published some while they were in Germany, and while she was translating Spinoza, but now, free from the constraints of translation, she had a new medium that gave fuller rein to the store of understanding developed over years of personal trial and devoted study. Even so, they required work. For example, the brilliant, justly celebrated essay on Dr. Cumming, the evangelical preacher, took two months of reading and writing. These essays gave her the latitude she had wanted, and encouraged her in a new kind of publication. Having read English and German literature, and a good bit of Italian and French, she put to use her self-taught knowledge of Greek and Latin by reading Sophocles, Aeschylus, Homer, Horace, Virgil, Cicero, Persius, Livy, Tacitus, Plautus, and Quintilian. She had plenty of time. Social ostracism was one cause, poverty another. The precariousness of their financial and professional circumstances absorbed considerable energy and attention. Living by one's pen is rarely a lucrative business, especially without the impulse fame gives to sales, and their interests were so diverse, their lodgings so temporary, that every ounce of attention must have been mustered just to meet the essentials. They were both tormented intermittently with bad health, often the result of stress, and they at the same time had to forgo even sixpenny luxuries. Still, they shared literature, and philosophy, they traveled to the seaside for George's studies of marine life, and wrote and corrected proofs. What it lacked in indulgences, their life even at this stage made up in interest and depth. She described herself at this time as "reading Homer and science and rearing tadpoles" (*Letters*, 2:202).

Vocation

Among her papers in Berlin, Marian had a brief fictional sketch she had written describing English village life. When she read it to George he encouraged her to try writing fiction, and three years later, in 1858, she finished the first of her three *Scenes of Clerical Life* ("The Sad Fortunes of Rev. Amos Barton"). They decided that George would contact John Blackwood, publisher of *Blackwood's Magazine* and a man whose tactful manners and principled business habits made him a favorite with many Victorian luminaries. Lewes, who had published there, wrote on behalf of "a friend who desires my good offices with you." This "clerical friend" wishes to remain anonymous, and will use the pseudonym, "George Eliot." The reasons for the anonymity are obvious enough. Anonymous reviewing was a policy at *Westminster*, so in publishing her essays there she had no choices to make. Her relationship with Lewes was widely known and disapproved, even in intellectual circles, and this reputation would pose an insurmountable obstacle to fair reception with the wider public for whom she wrote. It was probably not Marian's sensitivity alone that encouraged her husband to preserve her anonymity. The simple fact was that an outraged reception could very well have put an early end to her career as a novelist. Sensitivity was more than balanced by ambition. She wanted her fiction to be read and appreciated, and a pseudonym was essential to this end.[14]

When the second and third stories were written ("Mr. Gilfil's Love Story," and "Janet's Repentance") they, too, were drawn from Marian's childhood memories of the Midlands countryside, but enhanced as always by careful notes on such subjects as when flowers bloom in the Midlands, kinds of trees, the clergy, poverty of curates, multiple church "livings." The three stories were published in monthly installments in 1857, running from January to November, and they then appeared in two volumes in 1858. The reception was immediate and positive. The reviews were full of praise for the naturalness and truth of her portraits, and good responses came from the presentation copies sent by Blackwood to well-known persons like Dickens and Carlyle, whose interest might forward sales. Her re-

sponse to this success was characteristically diffident, trained as she
had been in the changeableness of opinion, but there is no doubt that
she felt a new epoch was beginning, and a new vocation opening before her.

Adam Bede, her first novel, was originally planned as a fourth clerical "Scene," but, she wrote to Blackwood (pseudononymously) that
she was "inclined to take a large canvas for it and write a novel" (*Letters*, 2:381, 387). She began it in October 1857, completed most of
volume 2 in the summer of 1858 while they were on a five-month
tour of Germany and Austria, and finished the sixth and final book
back in England. The subscription by circulating libraries was disappointing—only 50 copies for Mudies, the largest—and George was
worried. The publication had been delayed, the incognito was already
wearing thin, and, as he rightly calculated, the reviews would be savage were Marian known to be the author. Made alive to these dangers, Blackwood decided to publish all at once, not in magazine
installments, and by February 1859 it was out in three volumes. It
sold 5,000 copies in a fortnight, and the reviews with one exception
were full of praise. George Eliot immediately took her place in the
front rank of living novelists. Blackwood paid well for the work, a
tender of his future handsome treatment of his now famous author,
and the days of cheap lodgings were over.[15]

Her incognito, initially so important a protection, soon became a
liability and had to be dropped. Almost immediately rumors began
to circulate. John Chapman hinted to George that Marian was the author but Lewes gave him a frozen response. No sooner was that leak
dammed up than others appeared. She had revealed herself to Blackwood during the negotiations for *Adam Bede*, and he was unlikely to
break the confidence; but she had also revealed herself to Herbert
Spencer, during the publication of *Scenes of Clerical Life*, and he occasionally was careless of the secret in conversation. All this might have
been supportable, had it not been for the Liggins affair. A rural fellow named Joseph Liggins claimed he was George Eliot, produced
some forged manuscript as evidence, and complained Blackwood
never paid him a cent. Several champions appeared among rural curates and magistrates and some even appeared in better-dressed circles; charity collections were taken up for Liggins. This went on for
over a year, and when the story appeared in the *Times* it could not be
ignored. Spencer continued careless, Chapman was spreading the rumor in literary circles, and Liggins was on the march focusing atten-

tion on the pseudonym. She finally told her closest friends when it was clear there would be no protecting anonymity. As word rapidly spread she had to endure the inevitable pains of exposure, for example, the publication of a savage personal attack in the *Athenaeum*.

Her response to the ruckus was, typically, to take a ten-day vacation in Switzerland, something she and Lewes routinely did from this time on as a break from the stress of their work, carried on as it was with vigor but in a peculiar social isolation. Though she had good friends and old friends, circumstances created distance between even her and Barbara Bodichon, who did not live nearby, and Sara Hennell, whose loyalty remained constant but whose mind did not grow at the same pace as Marian's. She and Marian had conversed and written on problems suggested by the title of Sara's essay, "Christianity and Infidelity," but while Sara remained intent on such issues, Marian had moved from Feuerbach and Spinoza, to the *Westminster Review* essays and beyond, to her art. The peculiar combined strains of solitude and productivity often overstressed both the Leweses, but now Marian's financial success as an author made it possible for them to find the most congenial relief possible in travel to Italy, France, Germany, Spain, and the English country and seaside.

The Mill on the Floss (1860) was written partly on trips around the English countryside. During these weeks Marian stayed in their quiet lodgings to write while Lewes pursued his studies of marine life. Back in London she continued writing while she negotiated with Blackwood for the publication of her second novel. This writing cost her some personal sorrow, being based more closely on her own life than any other of her fictions. She waited anxiously to learn Blackwood's response to the first volume and worried about the quality and value of her work as she did it. Her ambition was such that she cared deeply for excellence; expressed in her letters many times is the view that the greatest accomplishment is to do whatever one does well, and the greatest sin is to do work for which one is unsuited. Her negotiations with Blackwood were a bit cool for a time when it became clear that he wanted the book for less than she rightly thought it deserved. However, George's long experience with such negotiations and her own long experience in publishing carried the day and Blackwood, partly against his brother's objection, settled on acceptable terms as to publication form and payment. Her chief anxiety apart from money was the proper format in which to present her work. Charles Dickens had made a near-revolution in publishing by issuing his novels in serial parts, but George Eliot's work developed differently than his, in terms less of plot than of accumulated conditions, so that small parts seemed to her to compromise the desired effect. Despite the extra money that serial publication promised, she held firm for publication in three volumes.

Before they had finished correcting proofs they had left on a journey to Italy, by way of Paris and Switzerland. They spent three and one-half months traveling from Naples and Genoa to Rome, Florence, Pisa, Venice, Verona, and other cities, stopping in the Alps to meet George's three sons at their boarding school, and at Geneva to see her old friends the D'Albert Durades. George's oldest son, Charles, came back to London with them, in preparation for a career in the colonies; Thornton, his second son, soon followed; and after a time the youngest, Bertie, also came home to London. Marian's relation with all three of her stepsons seems to have been one of mutual affection and respect. Partly to accommodate the boys, she and George rented a house for three years beginning that summer of 1860, and for the first time in a long time they stopped moving from one rented lodging to another. She was now "at home" more than ever before, and had to consider how to manage her obvious social difficulties. The social hostility to George and Marian because of their living situation was never total, and it crumbled slowly over the years. Still, to protect herself from the possibility of endless unpleasantness and pain she made it a firm policy never to make calls. Whoever saw her came *to* her, so neither the presence or absence of invitations nor the responsibility to make social calls became an important issue. This was obviously wise considering the extensive hostility they faced even in their families. Although George's mother thawed early, Marian's own family to the last man and woman, and despite the fact that she took George's name and the obligations of a married woman, never spoke to her again during Lewes's lifetime. Such hostility at home could not entirely be overcome by the news that the queen was reading her books aloud to the prince consort and thought them wonderful.

During her first Italian journey she had conceived an idea of writing a novel about Savonarola, the powerful religious leader of Renaissance Florence. After some initial work on the novel, however, another story forced itself into her attention and she wrote a short work, *Silas Marner*, in 1861, along with some other stories, before she returned to her next novel in earnest, taking a month in Florence to continue her research. Blackwood never negotiated for this novel because another publisher, George Smith of Cornhill's, made what Lewes called "the most magnificent offer ever yet made for a novel."[16] The offer of ten-thousand pounds probably deserves Lewes's description. *Romola* differs from her other novels in two respects; it was not published by Blackwood, and it was published in fourteen parts, beginning in July 1862 and running in *Cornhill Magazine* until December 1863, coming out thereafter in the customary three volumes. It was not a financial success for Cornhill, perhaps partly because of the circumstances of its publication (see below, chapter 4). It was a difficult novel for George Eliot to write, involving her in frequent trips to the country and seashore to escape the pressures she imposed on herself in order to write it; nevertheless, it contains some of her best work in her own opinion, and certainly marks a new phase in her writing in which she moves away from rural English life to a wider context.

Her own social circumstances were also changing. Always worried about money in the past because of their dependents, especially the three boys and Agnes, she now no longer had to write for money. Her successes were beginning to be translated into investments. Her social circle still included old friends like Barbara Bodichon and Mrs. Congreve, Sara and Cara, and the feminists Bessie Parkes and Mrs. Peter Taylor; but the circle was constantly widening to include more artists, scientists, and intellectuals—for example, Robert Browning; E. S. Dallas, the critic; Owen Jones, the architect who decorated the Crystal Palace interiors; Wilkie Collins; and Charles Darwin, Alfred Tennyson, eventually Turgenev, as well as members of various colleges at Oxford and Cambridge. In these changing conditions there seems to be a growing disproportion between her public life of recognition and acclaim and her private life, where she was still plagued with illness related partly to stress and anxiety about her work. The explanation for this seems not to lie with marital problems or professional worry so much as with the lifelong disability that her unique powers always seemed to entail. The picture is too incomplete to make a basis for responsible interpretation. There are conflicting reports concerning her shyness, and conflicting evidence concerning the effects of George's habit of deflecting bad reviews and negative reactions. There is little doubt that he treated her generously, sacrificing his work to help her; and this generosity had always been mutual, with Marian helping him through illness and with work deadlines. There is a possibility that Lewes's hovering contributed to her deep

discouragements by keeping her from active response to potential an-
tagonists. An unreliable witness like Edith Simcox claims that Lewes
alone made it possible for her to write fiction, and the claim has been
taken up and perpetuated. The evidence does not suggest that,
though the firmest evidence suggests a constant and close collaboration between Marian and George on all matters: those concerning his
Physiology of Common Life, his *Life of Goethe*, and his *Problems of Life
and Mind* (the ambitious work he left unfinished at the end of his life)
as well as those concerning her novels. Their collaboration, however,
does not diminish the independence of their minds and their work,
and was in fact a collaboration made possible by that independence.

The kind of poison that George tried to protect her from but that
indirectly kept being injected into her life is best grasped through an
anecdote about John Morley, who tried to enlist her, late in her career
and at the height of her fame, as an author in the English Men of
Letters Series for Macmillan. She considered it briefly, and of his
lunch with her he wrote to a colleague: "It is clear that our *Prima
Donna* must be paid on a different scale from the others—whether 3
or 5 times we must consider and consult." This nasty little innuendo,
and the attitude it implies, is evident indirectly in this unctuous note
he wrote a day or two later to George Eliot after she had decided to
refuse: "I feel as if the sun had gone out of the sky, editorially
speaking, since yesterday. It would have made such a difference in the
spirits and good heart of us all, if you had consented to lead us" (*Letters*, 6:416, notes 3–4). The fawning hypocrisy of the latter note,
which together with the ill-natured condescension of the first convey
a sense of the contempt and hostility that George Eliot had to deal
with all her life, and which appears to pass with Morley for gentle-
manly behavior.

Their circumstances changed again when they finally bought their
own house, The Priory, in November of 1863 and began receiving
people regularly for music and talk on weekends, first on Saturday
nights and later on Sunday afternoons. Among the new friends, for
example, was Theodore Martin, who came to be introduced and soon
brought his wife, Helen Faucit, a well-known tragic actress. After a
two-month holiday in Italy and France, Marian began working on a
verse drama called *The Spanish Gypsy*, and she kept writing and studying Spanish and enduring agonies of doubt concerning her ability to
write Shakespearean blank verse until George took the manuscript
away from her. Lewes's own affairs were busy as usual. His own scien-

tific work and writing went forward, earning him the respect of the best scientists, and at the same time he continued his literary activities, which at this time included editorial work at *Cornhill* magazine and the editorship of the *Fortnightly Review*.

In February 1865 Marian's journal records the beginning of a new novel, *Felix Holt, the Radical* (1866). A year after this first notice George sent volume 1 to Smith, who declined it, and then to Blackwood, who immediately closed the deal. From then on, the good relations between John Blackwood and his famous author remained secure. The novel was published in three volumes, as were the first two, and Marian and Lewes were soon off again for three months of work and travel. Returning in 1866, they left again early in 1867 because of Lewes's health and had ten weeks of strenuous travel and walking in Germany. Lewes returned looking and feeling hardier, and Marian returned to the unfinished *Spanish Gypsy*, a work certainly informed by her knowledge of Spinoza. This time she finished and Blackwood published it in 1868, just before another trip to Germany for several weeks in the mountains. Poetry was not George Eliot's strong suit, and despite their intellectual interest her long poems are not exciting reading, not even *The Spanish Gypsy* with its background in the Spanish Inquisition and its interesting questions about the nature of freedom. She wrote other narrative poems and a sonnet sequence during the next two years, but throughout her blank verse seems heavy and formless. One wishes for more of her satiric couplets, which by comparison seem effortless and accomplished. However, the ferment that produced this poetry was preparing a great event. By 1869 she had begun work on *Middlemarch* (1872), the novel that many have considered her masterpiece.

Middlemarch got on slowly at first. She was taking notes and writing poetry, and dodging English travelers abroad during a trip to Germany and Italy. Some of her notes from this trip made their way into *Middlemarch*. In Rome she and George met an Englishwoman, Mrs. William Cross, and her son John Walter Cross, a man who was soon to be a close companion at the Priory, to be their broker in charge of investments, and eventually to be even more closely related to Marian. At home, other troubles distracted them from work. In 1869 Thornie returned from Natal, where he had gone in 1863 like other ambitious young Englishmen and where he had been joined by his brother, Bertie, in 1866. After six years Thornie was back very ill, much thinner and in considerable pain. The foremost doctor was sent for, who seems to have misdiagnosed the condition for over a month, and then a specialist finally indicated Thornie had an incurable glandular tuberculosis. After six months at the Priory, where he was nursed by the Leweses, Thornie died in October 1869, at the age of twenty-five. The experience cut deeper than George Eliot could have guessed, as she told a correspondent. She was still unable to get back to work on her big novel. Lewes's own illnesses then sent them to Germany for two months in the spring of 1870, and again to the English coast soon after their return home. During this time she wrote Blackwood that Middlemarch "creeps on" (Letters, 5:99). By Christmas that year the first book, "Miss Brooke," was well along. When she finally finished the novel in 1872 Blackwood published it in eight parts, one for each of the eight books it contained. This new format, a compromise between the three-volume simultaneous publication and the serial publication in many parts, was a great success and was the format she and Blackwood used for her next (it turned out to be her last) novel.

Back from a month in Germany she was met with an astonishing critical reception. Middlemarch was famous. Its impact was enormous. Even Herbert Spencer was expansive. The outpouring of letters and gifts from all parts of the world was unprecedented even for her. Though she accepted very few invitations, she was now invited to dinner. Lewes reports to Blackwood the following telling anecdote: "Mad. Bodichon wrote to her the other day that Judge Fitzgerald told her at the opening of the Dublin Exhibition he was struck with the attention of the Archbishop to the interior of his hat which at first he took for devout listening to the speeches, but on close examination saw he was reading something, and as this was so intent he was prompted to look also into the hat, and found the Archbishop had Middlemarch there laid open . . ." (Letters, 5:291).

Another trip to Germany preceded the first sketches of her next novel, Daniel Deronda (1872), published like Middlemarch in eight parts. This novel demonstrates especially clearly her habit of moving on from an achievement to explore new problems. In this work she takes up her contemporary London society and the wider world in which it coexists with so many other systems, systems that to the English seem "foreign." The ideas and vision that inspired her first fiction are evident in the last; but in Daniel Deronda her continual experiments in form are most evident. She wrote much of it in considerable pain from kidneystones, but in considerable peace as well, having taken a house in the country for four months during the summer of 1874, where she and George could work uninterrupted by Sunday callers. Again the next summer, they spent June through September in the country leaving only to visit the dentist and meet Queen Victoria. More bad news from Natal left them again troubled deeply. Bertie had died, possibly of the same disease as Thornie. Coping with this shock they struggled to keep working. Her novel was finished in June 1876, and she and George left again for the Continent, both ill. The public acclaim kept growing. Royalty asked to be introduced; letters arrived from all over the world with expressions of personal gratitude for her work; in circles where people once took Agnes's part against her there were now rumors that Lewes's first wife was insane; hangers-on like Edith Simcox appeared (Edith attached herself to Marian after reviewing *Middlemarch* for a journal and could be shaken off only with difficulty). The need for quiet was more urgent than ever; in 1876 with John Cross's help they bought Witley Heights for their summers in the country. Though plagued increasingly with illness, they went there gratefully in June and spent four peaceful months in the summer of 1877 and again in the summer of 1878.

The next November (1878) things fell apart with a single unexpected blow. While the servants went to London to open the Priory they went to Brighton, where Lewes had a severe attack of pain. The doctor came, Cross left his own mother's death-bed, but George could not be saved. He died on 29 November, and a stunned Marian went into seclusion. Three months later she was still seeing no one, though she wrote to John Cross: "The perpetual mourner—the grief that can never be healed—is innocently enough felt to be wearisome by the rest of the world. And my sense of desolation increases" (*Letters*, 7:102). She set aside her own work and undertook the large share of their correspondence and negotiations with publishers and the public that had formerly fallen to Lewes. She was his executor, though it must have been a painful reminder of their struggles, for her to use the locution that, for legal purposes, enrolled her as "Mary Ann Evans, spinster." Herself ill, she worked on his unpublished manuscript, *Problems of Life and Mind*, refusing to return to her own work until it was published. She relied on John Cross in financial matters as Lewes and she both had done for some years, but she otherwise saw little company. Long accustomed to the companionship of Lewes in work and pleasure, in travel, in daily reading aloud, in correcting

proofs, and in discussing new projects, she must have felt his loss se-
verely and in every dimension of her life. She was aware that solitude
was not supportable or healthy, but she emerged from it only very
slowly over the next year and a half.

Finally, at the end of this period, she and John Cross married. It
is very difficult thoroughly to understand her motives, though some
have not been slow to speculate. Her need for companionship and
support, cultivated over long years of intimacy with Lewes, may have
prompted her to reach out; she may, in her grief and the profusion of
other burdens that accompanied it, have simply wanted help and
company. Cross had already proposed marriage twice before in the period after Lewes's death and been put off. Whatever the invisible history of this event, however, the marriage shocked her friends as her
earlier common-law marriage had shocked them, although the individual friends differed in each case. A formal letter arrived from
brother Isaac, breaking his silence of twenty-five years, congratulating
her on her marriage (and hence, on her first respectability in his eyes).

They bought a house at 4 Cheyne Walk and in May 1880 left on
a wedding trip to Paris and Italy. They returned in midsummer to a
fairly normal life of work and visiting; but from the time of Lewes's
death and despite efforts to take up life again on new terms, there is
a sense of oppression and dreariness in her letters that never really
vanishes. Then, just as suddenly as she had lost George, John Cross
lost her. They had begun attending Sunday concerts again at St.
James Hall, and after the concert of 19 December 1880, she complained of a cold. She got worse rapidly and she died on 22 December. The doctor reported irregular heart activity after listening with
his stethoscope, and John Cross reported that her last words were an
attempt to communicate the presence of severe pain in her left side.

She was refused burial in Westminster Abbey by a pious dean, and
was buried in Highgate Cemetery beside George Henry Lewes.

Chapter Two
Intellectual Mainstream: The Translations and Essays

The single most useful work for interpreting George Eliot's novels is Ludwig Feuerbach's astonishing, groundbreaking *Das Wesen des Christentums* (1841), translated and published by Marian Evans as *The Essence of Christianity* (1854) on the eve of her departure for Europe with Lewes. Hers remains the definitive English translation. Of the vast reading that informs her work, *The Essence of Christianity* ranks with Spinoza's *Ethics* as the most important introduction to her humane and original conception of human freedom.

Feuerbach

Although she had already translated David Friedrich Strauss's 1836 work *Das Leben Jesu* (published as *The Life of Jesus*, 1846), and although Strauss had a signal role in her intellectual maturing, he did not go far enough for George Eliot toward freeing moral life from some transcendental reality and from the negative constraints it entailed. Like Feuerbach, she deliberately moved well beyond Strauss's Hegelian idea of "transcendental spirit" or collective mind of humanity. Of this Straussian notion one critic rightly says:

> Nothing could be more alien than this to the mature thought of George Eliot, with its secular emphasis upon the concrete, the human, the particular. It is precisely the Hegelian approach of Strauss that Feuerbach is attacking when he seeks to resolve metaphysics into psychology, theology into anthropology. Feuerbach completely reverses the procedure of Hegel and Strauss.[1]

For George Eliot it is precisely the absence of a unifying transcendental reality that most gives importance to human choice and action. In Feuerbach she found a mind more venturesome even than Strauss, and more in harmony with her own.

Feuerbach's usefulness extends beyond his limited application as a
gloss for the novels. It is true that many pages in *The Essence of Christianity*, especially because it is translated in her own words, prefigure
some passage in George Eliot's fiction. This one, for example, suggests the portrait of Mrs. Tulliver in *The Mill on the Floss*:

It is a sign of an undiscriminating good nature, a womanish instinct, to
gather together and then to preserve tenaciously all that we have gathered,
not to trust anything to the waves of forgetfulness, to the chance of memory,
in short not to trust ourselves and learn to know what really has value for
us.[2]

However, taking this as an apt description of Mrs. Tulliver's main
impulse in responding to pressure raises problems of other kinds. The
phrase "womanish instinct," for example, with all it implies, is not
necessarily one that George Eliot would have chosen, given her keen
awareness of sexist biases in language and custom. Any reading of
George Eliot in the light of Feuerbach must constantly allow for the
constraints of translation. In the end, Feuerbach is most useful for his
general conception of human experience; and in this role his work offers a vocabulary and method for approaching George Eliot's own
work that is more fruitful than approaches derived from positions foreign to her conceptions: positions, for example, presuming a conflict
between morality and realism and various other versions of the
"warmed-over Christianity" theme that has vitiated George Eliot criticism. It is exactly the large conception of Feuerbach's work, the
daring anthropological approach to Christianity, that first attracted
Marian Evans and that provided corroboration for her own belief in
the inseparability of moral and material issues.

Strauss was a natural introduction to Feuerbach's philosophy, just
as Charles Bray and Charles Hennell were natural introductions to
Strauss.[3] All three turned their attention to the German revolution
in metaphysics and theology. The motivating perception behind this
revolution, as it appears in George Eliot's work at least, is the perception that absolute moral authority actually destroys moral vigor by
encouraging passivity. In her novels personal honor and moral
strength develop by exercise; and there is no freedom of exercise
(through choice, consequence, vision and revision) where dogmatic
truth has tranquillized the moral system with certainties. In his particular development of this motive Feuerbach's work involves a step

of profound methodological importance; that is, the insistent refusal to separate ideas and things. It is not a difficult step in itself, but it seems counterintuitive because, as George Eliot says in a different context, it goes against the entire drift of Western philosophy from Parmenides to Kant.[4] Among other things, it points to the self-reflexiveness of human meaning. The originality of this move will be most evident in examples from Feuerbach's work where we can see, in Marian Evans's translation, what such a move means intuitively and practically.

Feuerbach's preface to *The Essence of Christianity* gives some sense of the boldness of his work and of the stir it generated. He says his work is not for schools but for mankind, not for theological dispute but for human understanding; it reaches beyond doctrine and dogma to "the very core of religion," affirming the human value of dedication and belief. "The new philosophy can no longer, like the old Catholic and modern Protestant scholasticism, fall into the temptation to prove its agreement with religion by its agreement with religious dogmas." Dogma, in fact, belongs to "the false or theological essence of religion" (the phrase is his title for part 1 of *The Essence*), while "the true or theological essence of religion" (his title for part 2) exists in action: in the individual exercise of love, humanity, service, creativity, repentance. It is religion, not dogma and institutional theologies, that carries the true Spirit; and that Spirit is not supernatural, not foreign to human nature, but wholly central to it. "I by no means say," he insists, "God is nothing, the Trinity is nothing, the work of God is nothing, &c. I only show that they are not that which the illusions of theology make them,—not foreign, but native mysteries, the mysteries of human nature" (*Essence*, ch. 38). Feuerbach interprets theology as human expressions of aspiration, a reservoir of human achievement, and hence a basis for action, not a command to passivity.

Two examples from his argument may make his method plainer (another example appears in chapter 4 below). The first is his discussion of "The Mystery of the Incarnation," where he connects the scientific and the religious spirit, and where he concludes that the formula "God is love" really means "Love is God," that is, an ideal of human achievement at its highest and best.

Religion has its basis in the essential difference between man and the brute—the brutes have no religion. . . . But what is this most essential difference between man and the brute? The most simple, general, and the most popular answer to this question is—consciousness: *but consciousness in the strict sense . . . {is} present only in a being to whom his species, his essential nature, is an object of thought. . . .* Where there is this higher consciousness there is a capability of science. Science is the cognizance of species." (pp. 1–2; pt. 1, ch. 1) (italics mine).

So, for example, the Mystery of the Incarnation is a practical manifestation of the human nature of God—human nature taken collectively in its achievements and potentialities.

Thus if God loves man, man is the heart of God—the welfare of man his deepest anxiety. If man, then, is the object of God, is not man, in God, an object to himself? Is not the content of the divine nature the human nature? If God is love, is not the essential content of this love man? Is not the love of God to man—the basis and central point of religion—the love of man to himself made an object, contemplated as the highest objective truth, as the highest being to man? Is not then the proposition, "God loves man" an orientalism (religion is essentially oriental), which in plain speech means, the highest is the love of man?" (p. 58; pt. 1, ch. 4)

The whole interpretation rests on one's ability to see oneself as a member of a species. Each individual, to use the language of his first chapter, is "at once I and Thou"; each can put himself or herself in the place of another because of the essentially human power to think, not merely about individual existence, but about essential nature. All qualities predicated of the species, for example, its ideals as expressed in Christianity, are qualities that have been attributed to "God"; but these ideals—loving, suffering, immortality, for example—are really qualities of the human subject taken not individually but collectively.

   A second example of Feuerbach's argument, with its characteristic reversal of subject and predicate, is the discussion of the "Mystery of the Suffering God":

God suffers—suffering is the predicate—but for men, for others, not for himself. What does that mean in plain speech? Nothing else than this: to suffer for others is divine; he who suffers for others, who lays down his life for them, acts divinely, is a God to men.

   The Passion of Christ, however, represents not only moral voluntary suffering, the suffering of love, the power of sacrificing the self for the good of others; it represents also suffering as such, suffering in so far as it is an expression of possibility in general. (p. 60; pt. 1, ch. 5)

In other words, the worship of sorrow, as expressed in the Christian religion, is the expression of the high value placed on the powers of endurance and receptivity: not only the "voluntary suffering" but also "passibility" or sensibility, receptiveness, feeling, even weakness, in general.

These two examples cannot be taken out of context except with extreme caution; they are not portable maxims, especially for application to George Eliot, who certainly does not share all of Feuerbach's views. For example, if what is understood by "sacrificing the self" is abandonment of ego (there is some question whether this is what Feuerbach means), then the view certainly conflicts with the vision of George Eliot, whose novels demonstrate repeatedly that sympathy—the recognition of the "Thou" by the "I"—is impossible without ego. In selecting these two examples from Feuerbach, my intention is for one demonstration only: that Feuerbach explores the teaching and doctrine of Christianity as representations by mankind *of* itself, *to* itself. His *Essence of Christianity* is presented as a monologue of the Voice of Human Nature. Marian Evans's choice to translate Feuerbach demonstrates how important she felt his work to be, and how in sympathy with her own understanding she found his effort. It is this general emphasis, not particular passages or extractable maxims, that offer the serious reader of George Eliot the most suggestive evidence. Influence is one part of a dynamic process, a fact especially plain in George Eliot's relation to everything she read. Speaking of Carlyle's influence, for example, she wrote:

It has been well said that the highest aim in education is analogous to the highest aim in mathematics, namely, to obtain not *results* but *powers*, not particular solutions, but the means by which endless solutions may be wrought.

In a writer, such an influence is dynamic. "He does not, perhaps, enrich your stock of data, but he clears away the film from your eyes that you may search for data to some purpose" (*Essays*, 213). Feuerbach's perception that existence and essence are one, his refusal to accept prevailing transcendental notions, and his ability to conceive of a morally, socially disciplined and principled existence quite apart from such transcendental notions, had great appeal to George Eliot, an author who, like Feuerbach, gives back to religion and to the language of moral force a personal voice.

The reunion of ideas and things has central importance in George Eliot's work, and is explored further elsewhere.[5] Three corollaries of this central idea deserve mention here. All of them bear on George Eliot's idea of the *social* universe, something not addressed explicitly by Feuerbach. Her idea of the social universe involves: 1) its separation from nature, that is, its artificiality; 2) its roots in tradition, and; 3) its dependence on individual creativity. First, the separation of human culture from nature is an essential premise behind the anthropological approach to human nature. Everything human—from private tastes to institutional dogmas—belongs to a free universe, not one inherent in and dependent upon the natural universe with its divine or its deterministic laws. Culture has its own systematic principles (laws), and hence its own inexorable order of causes and consequences; but whatever their definition, they are always the residue of human rather than nonhuman agency, and thus they are always available to human influence. Belief in nonhuman sources of order means relieving humanity of its responsibility: a belief she characterized as "the phantasmagoria of hope unsustained by reason" (*Letters*, 2:49). Expressing late in her career a recognizably Feuerbachian idea, she wrote, "the idea of Good, so far as it has been a high spiritual influence, is the Ideal of a goodness entirely human (i.e., an exaltation of the human)" (*Letters*, 6:98). One excellent way of considering George Eliot's much-discussed narrator is as a representation of the self-awareness of the human species.

Second, the root of culture is tradition, not nature. Tradition is its element, its determining and material condition. In the "historical life of all the world," she wrote to a fellow artist, "our little personal share of her seems a mere standing room from which we can look all round, and chiefly backward" (*Letters*, 5:391). Far from discouraging ambition, this situation fosters it. Culture is a kind of conservation, where influences live long after they have left the hand that shaped them; and the idea that nothing is lost is a source for George Eliot of "invigorating motive" (*Letters*, 4:158; 3:316). Tradition, furthermore, unlike nature, is full of contradictions, and exists only in continued acts of individuals, both personally and collectively. Tradition is an incarnate reality, not an abstraction existing apart from particulars. It is capable of metamorphosis and it is freighted with contradiction. Judaism and Hinduism coexist as uneasily as do libertarians and slave-owners; even in the same person, bigotry about race or sex may go hand in hand with highly cultivated taste. Her essay on "The

Antigone and Its Moral" puts succinctly and eloquently the mixed nature of all human experience, and the need of daring for accomplishment.

Preach against false doctrines, you disturb feeble minds and send them adrift on a sea of doubt; make a new road, and you annihilate vested interests; cultivate a new region of the earth, and you exterminate a race of men. Wherever the strength of a man's intellect or moral sense, or affection brings him into opposition with the rules which society has sanctioned, there is renewed the conflict between Antigone and Creon; such a man must not only dare to be right, he must also dare to be wrong—to shake faith, to wound friendship, perhaps, to hem in his own powers. (*Essays,* 264–65)

This often-quoted statement has, among its suggestions, the implication that conflict is inevitable to growing life, as it breaks through limits and repudiates finality; and the alternative implication that the appearance of success, or failure, is always relative.[6]

Third, and following as a result from its autonomous and mixed nature, culture continues only through individual creativity. The simplest observance of a tradition renews it and hence is partly creative; even the lack of such observance has the power of weakening a tradition; both acts alter the balance of influence. The most original creativity consolidates in new forms what has not yet been imagined or achieved. Genius itself is a power of action, "consisting neither in self-conceit nor in humility, but in a power to make or do, not anything in general, but something in particular."[7] In *Daniel Deronda* the terrible Klesmer bears in upon the faltering heroine, emphasizing the difficulty, and power, and importance of deliberate action, as opposed to the lazy sloppiness of most daily affairs. "You are a beautiful young lady—you have been brought up in ease—you have done what you would—you have not said to yourself, 'I must know this exactly,' 'I must understand this exactly,' 'I must do this exactly' "—three terrible "musts" for a young lady who combines a generalized burning ambition with particular habits of the most conventional sort.

Creativity, furthermore, is something that is only possible in a human, social context; the solitary creator is more a mad thing than a creative influence. Science, for example, "is the cognizance of the species" to Feuerbach; as such it is a fully moral activity to the extent that it maintains the species-consciousness, the link between I and Thou that divides humanity from the "brutes." In both Feuerbach and George Eliot we can find the interesting perception of a link, rather than a competition, between science and poetry. Both are moral because both are species-conscious activities, and both are thus humanly grounded, invented activities. Both are part of culture, and consequently both are linked in principle against the solipsism and subjectivity of supernaturalism. Early Christianity "cared nothing for the species, and had only the individual in its eye and mind" (*Essence*, p. 151; pt. 1, ch. 16); likewise, the atheist or agnostic, or the radical individualist (what she calls the philistine) is in the same unquestioning condition; even the custom-bound peasant of whatever class remains ignorant of the species because he or she is unaware of differences between individuals. Self and Other, I and Thou are born together in Western philosophy and neither alone has secure reality. No wonder that in George Eliot's work neither alone is a basis for fully human life. In culture (as George Eliot conceives it) is achieved a balance of those forces whereby individual effort and traditional wisdom maintain creative tension. Outside them is a darkness that amounts to the death of what is most human.[8]

Spinoza

When Marian Evans began translating Spinoza's *Ethics* in 1854 she had just published her translation of Feuerbach and departed from London bound for Germany with George Henry Lewes. She began the first two parts in Berlin, she finished part 3 at Dover on their return, while Lewes went to London to look for lodging and to scout their social circumstances, and she finished parts 4 and 5 at Richmond, early in 1856. She certainly chose Spinoza's work for its independent value, but at this particular time the task had a special personal value for her as a kind of meditation, a support for her mind and feeling and a focus for her attention during the period of greatest trauma over her break with her family and with social convention.

She already knew Spinoza's work well. In an 1849 letter to Sara Hennell she wrote that she was translating Spinoza's political treatise, the *Tractatus Theologico-politicus*. She may have read the articles Lewes had published on Spinoza before she met him; she certainly read Froude's, which she praised as an "admirable summary" (*Letters*, 2:211). But her discovery of Spinoza was not idiosyncratic. The German romantics, especially Goethe, as well as Lewes, Froude, and others in England, all found in Spinoza a major statement for the nineteenth century. When they returned to England, Lewes, who had published on Spinoza, undertook to arrange with Bohn for the publication of her translation. The unhappy conclusion of this effort, largely it appears through impolitic negotiation about money by an unbelieveably harried and harrassed Lewes, was a severe blow to Marian, despite her long-standing awareness that it would never bring her much fortune. How severe the blow was can be guessed from her conspicuous silence on the subject from beginning to end, and from the fact that she never again tried to see it published. The recent publication of this translation is an inestimable service to George Eliot's readers and to cultural historians.[9]

With Spinoza, as with Feuerbach, George Eliot's views agree in some respects and not in others; so again, in considering the relations of the *Ethics* to her fiction the question of influence is best answered by looking for emphases and directional signals, rather than for equations between their views. And questions of influence seem somewhat peripheral, considering that Marian Evans had developed to maturity before she translated the *Ethics*. In translating it she was making available in English a work she considered major. She had translated Strauss and Feuerbach, and had written some of her most important essays (including for example more than half of the essays included in Thomas Pinney's standard collection); having got this far intellectually and productively, she turned to Spinoza as an autonomous intelligence acknowledging an ally. Although Spinoza is generally regarded as an elegant, subtle, hard-to-classify philosopher, his difficulty typically does not deter her. It is characteristic of her that she went directly to the essential sources, regardless of their controversiality or difficulty. She simply proceeded to learn the language necessary to read him (in this case medieval Latin), and made him accessible to her English compatriots.

Spinoza can be considered a foremost philosopher of freedom.[10] Although his work requires some discipline in the reader, its difficulty can be overstated. It is readable, and not inaccessible to an educated intelligence; but one grasps him as much by intuition as by total clarity of logic, despite his relentlessly logical (even geometrical) form. And this, Spinoza might say, is as it should be, given the importance in his system of intuition. He goes far beyond the relatively mechanical models of Cartesian philosophy and far beyond what Feuerbach calls "vulgar empiricism" (*Essence*, p. 11; pt. 1, ch. 1). He imagines the human mind and its conditions on the model of "systems within systems, each with its own characteristic equilibrium of forces."[11] His appeal for the late-eighteenth- and nineteenth-century writer was at least partly inspired by his political ideas, which were published nearly two centuries before their time; a century and a half before the American Constitution, with which his thought shares a spirit.

Given the excitement that he knew the *Ethics* was bound to cause, Spinoza did not publish it in his lifetime. It appeared posthumously in the year of his death, 1677, and it is composed of five parts: 1) "Concerning God"; 2) "Of the Nature and Origin of the Mind"; 3) "On the Origin and Nature of the Emotions"; 4) "Of Human Bondage, or the Strength of the Emotions"; and 5) "On the Power of the Understanding, or of Human Freedom." Crucial to his entire theory of knowledge is a doctrine of two worlds, one divine and one human. The divine creation or "Substance," he holds, is a unity, but human existence, which is composed of *finite modes* of the Divine, is limited by its *modal* existence from ever completely perceiving the fullest truths of creation. Mind and body, for example, are parts of a oneness—they are "at once mind and body"[12]—but we can only know them separately, through different faculties (either of mind—through thought—or of body—through the characteristic motion and rest of physical bodies). Divine Substance (or Being, or God), being perfect, has no purpose; it is going nowhere, it needs nothing. Purpose is a feature of deficiency (that is, of human limitation), and therefore not part of the Perfect Being. The less purposive human activity is, therefore, the closer it is to divine Substance; the more there is of such activity, so defined, the less there is of purpose and deficiency. We live as part of a divine unity, but as modal (limited, deficient, not-perfect) creatures our faculties are divided, and so our perception of that unity is clouded. To perfect ourselves is to act more and more as what we are, part of divine Substance, and this is the basis for all social and political dealings among human beings.

The complexity of these views, the originality of his vision of freedom and purpose for religion, politics, and emotional or psychological theory, cannot be summarized briefly. Some of the most important implications for George Eliot's work, however, can be suggested. Most important of these is the spirit of tolerance that breathes largely through his work. He demonstrates vigorously the evil—the actual "malignancy"—of factionalism for all social and political and religious life. Arising from the inevitable prejudices of modal, finite existence, factionalism is an expression of confusion: confusion of what is perfect with what is not. It arises from the anthropomorphism that takes human desires for self-preservation and profit (just and reasonable things in Spinoza's view) and equates them with the absolute conditions of divine Substance, or God (not just and reasonable in Spinoza's view). Karl Jaspers characterizes Spinoza's position as follows:

Believing that the gods provide useful things in order to obligate men and so receive their highest veneration, men have devised different ways of worshipping God, each group in the hope that He will love them more than all the others. They imagine the gods and nature to be as insane as themselves.[13]

For Spinoza, Substance or Being simply *is*. It is going nowhere, because it is perfect and replete.

The "religion"—Christianity, for example—that conceives Substance in terms inappropriate to it (in terms of human limitation), falls into deficiency. One might call such Christianity a Secular Christianity, turning into deficient terms what is perfect, and doing so by losing the sense, always present in Spinoza, of the difference between human perception and the divine Substance. In ways that suggest affinities with Feuerbach and George Eliot, Spinoza suggests the destructive influence of such belief on the individual spirit and on political freedom. Such belief gives to the tools man invented for overcoming his imperfection—for example, to words, creeds, observances—the absolute status of God; the creed, not God, becomes absolute. Such is superstition in whatever form, and in all forms it generates hatred. It is divisive and dangerous, Spinoza holds, to a free society.[14] In the same spirit, Spinoza approaches the Bible, rejecting "all interpretations based on authority, regardless of where they originated."[15] No worldly authority is an exception to the laws limiting all human understanding, and all worldly authority is relevant only to a time or place, that is, to a mode of existence.

The free, or philosophical intellect, unlike those more bound by custom or impulse, can see the social value of even demonstrably shallow or erroneous views. Any view, because it exists at all, has some part in Substance and hence in what is valuable and permanent. All minds are bits of Substance, or God; all modal existence, however deficient, is a predicate of Substance. Spinoza's philosophy encourages a spirit of inclusiveness in which all finite beings are taken together, each with its particular contributing, if limited, value. All modal (human, finite) existence, even the most limited, must be tolerated; at the same time, all modal existence must limit its own exercise by recognizing its own limitations and avoiding any dogmatic and absolutist claims for what is so partial and deficient. The social order, says Spinoza, exists entirely to insure that this tolerance and restraint prevail.

Especially interesting, for purposes of reading George Eliot, is Spinoza's emphasis *against* purpose. Freedom from deficiency corresponds to the degree of freedom from purpose. The more free an individual is, the more value-free that individual's knowledge and the more independent of insistent, particular goals; freedom means intuiting the necessity of God, or Substance, and thus also the inevitable contingency and limitation of all finite human existence. Spinoza, like Feuerbach after him (Feuerbach often cites Spinoza), collapses the distinction between what is "right" and what "is," at the same time demonstrating that this means quite the opposite of moral laxity. The spirit of this position, complex through it is, can be suggested by a passage from George Eliot's essay on "The Natural History of German Life," where she reviews Riehl's argument concerning political organization among peasants:

The thing for mankind to know is, not what are the motives and influences which the moralist thinks *ought* to act on the labourer or the artisan, but what are the motives and influences which *do* act on him. (*Essays,* 271)

And, later in the same essay, *"a universal social policy,"* especially because it necessarily falsifies the diverse particulars of human experience and expression, *"has no validity except on paper"* (289). She quotes approvingly Riehl's statement that communism is "the despair of the individual in his own manhood, reduced to a system" (299). What "ought" to be is not a concern for a free individual. Although the question of what "is" remains problematic because perception is always subjective and partial, nevertheless, such qualified search for accuracy is a method that is preferable to dogmatic or purposive ones precisely because the question of truth remains problematic for finite human beings. The subjectivity of perception only invalidates perception if there is an alternative kind, some trustworthy absolute view; but there is no such thing in human life, no abstract right, or final true word, but only the sum of subjective truths working collectively in various corners of a vast, imperfectly comprehended human enterprise. The position being described here appears everywhere in George Eliot's work. Praising Goethe's "large tolerance," she writes that the distinction between right and wrong, "the line between the virtuous and the vicious, so far from being a necessary safeguard to morality, is itself an immoral fiction" (*Essays,* 147). In this belief she found a corroborative and powerful ally in Spinoza.

Seeing the similarities between George Eliot's views and Spinoza's requires, to be quite in their spirit, seeing their differences as well. As with Feuerbach, there are important differences. Spinoza's idea of necessity, based upon his conception of Absolute Substance or God, is not congenial to George Eliot, for whom all transcendence is historical, its laws determinate but not deterministic. Further, she separates completely the realms of nature and culture, thus liberating culture from necessity. Political and social life for Spinoza are embedded in nature, which he sees as a unity formed by Divine Substance. Finally, although she does distinguish between kinds of purpose, George Eliot stresses the importance of purpose. Having a guiding idea, like the idea of an artist or the hypotheses of a scientist, or even the ordinary person's vague desire to be better, is a means for shaping one's activity that reaches beyond immediate wants.

There are, however, some practical consequences of Spinoza's philosophy that have corresponding expression in George Eliot's work. First, there is a double principle in Spinoza of separation and unity; a very similar principle is articulated by George Eliot, most explicitly in her last novel (Daniel Deronda's vocation of "separateness with communication") but everywhere implicit in her aesthetic theory of form and in her view of moral life (see below the discussion of "The Morality of Art"). Second is Spinoza's faith in the efficacy of knowledge for achieving freedom. Because human unhappiness is a function of human deficiency, and human bondage to the finite, human happiness increases with the increased freedom from that bondage through knowledge. The more persons understand of their limits, the more they transcend them, and thus gain their freedom. This idea will be familiar to readers of George Eliot's fiction, and it is very far from the more familiar ideas that intellect (Reason) takes priority over emotion (Passion), or that consciousness gains control of impulse by depreciating the value or importance of impulse, emotion, or passion. Spinoza encourages the simultaneous, the unified exercise of both intellect and emotion together. Third, Spinoza stresses the value of activity. Evil, if there is such a thing for Spinoza, is passivity, banality, inactivity.

This view, like the desire to resist or contain fanaticism, rests on a belief in the creative power of individuals. The errors that are most evil are those that, by claiming superior truth, encourage passivitiy, complacency, rest. Activity is divine, passivity only the reflex of a being in bondage. Given his devaluation of purpose, such activity must be conceived in other than purposive terms, a possibility that George Eliot's moral ideal of aesthetic order may to some extent develop. In any case, and for Spinoza, the refusal to exercise one's powers, all one's powers, actively and fully is, like the refusal to hear an opponent, a denial of the primacy and sovereignty of God.[16]

A final affinity between Spinoza and George Eliot is biographical. In his own life Spinoza understood well the pain of disenfranchisement and the destructive power of orthodoxies. As a Jew, living in Spain during the Inquisition, he experienced the prejudice and persecution of that long reign of terror. But his experience went further. Not only was he persecuted by the Spanish Catholic church as Jew, he was persecuted by Jews in Holland (where his family had fled) for his resistance to orthodoxy. He was especially resistant to orthodoxy because of the passivity it encouraged, and when he was anathematized by his own synagogue (essentially driven out), he protested legally because, in the Dutch state, religious rights entailed certain political rights, and he especially valued his role as a citizen because of the opportunities for action it entailed. Doubly exiled for his views by both sides of an ideological opposition, he learned with special emphasis the limitations of orthodoxy. Neither dogmatic system could make room for his claims to freedom of thought and belief. (George Eliot's knowledge of Spinoza's life was undoubtedly part of the inspiration for her long poem called *The Spanish Gypsy*, which deals with the moral dilemmas and choices of those living during the Inquisition or, more generally, a time of conflicting claims to allegiance.)

George Eliot admired Spinoza's life, as do many, for its dignity, generosity, and rare discipline, but she must also have recognized in the seventeenth-century Jew's history a particular experience remarkably similar to her own. Prevented because of her sex from the professional and educational opportunities her culture opened to men, ostracized for her beliefs first by her father, and eventually by her relentless brother and by her society, she understood the power of exclusion and the malignancy of orthodoxies. She wrote scathingly against the "vulgarity of exclusiveness" of various social classes in England. Spinoza's work, a product of a similar experience, offered her a familiar voice and a meditation on the conditions of life as she knew it. Still, it is the spirit and not the letter of comparison that should remain uppermost. The similarities between her ideas and those of anyone else, including Spinoza, are always qualified and restrained by her own mature sense of truth. Speaking of John Henry Newman, the Anglican churchman notoriously turned Catholic at the cost of so much, she wrote in a vein that applied to all her potential influences: his autobiography "mainly affects me as the revelation of a life—how different in form from one's own, yet with how close a fellowship in its needs and burdens. . ." (*Letters,* 4:159). Despite particular differences from Spinoza she found in his work a common, passionate concern with the conditions of freedom.

Essays

George Eliot was still translating Spinoza when she began writing the series of essays that confirms her powers as a major writer. Most of them were published between 1855 and 1857 when she and Lewes needed money, although she did write and publish essays later in her career. She was writing these essays when she published her first fiction, *Scenes of Clerical Life,* and after she began to write her novels she published essays infrequently by comparison with this period in the mid 1850s. These essays are witty, conversational, informative, and altogether a pleasure to read. Together with the translations, and second only to the novels themselves, they provide the most reliable clues to the mature thought of the author. George Eliot's essays have always been eclipsed somewhat by her novels, but that is unfortunate; they are original and wide-ranging and deserve special attention. By their continued interest and relevance, moreover, they remind us of the similarities between her period and our own. The remainder of this chapter will deal briefly with the essays. First, two issues merit separate attention because they appear so often in different essays: the morality of art, and the unequal situation of women; following this, separate attention to five of her most important essays will serve to indicate the nature of her concerns and powers as a journalist.

The morality of art.   George Eliot's shift from ethics to aesthetics is one of the most eloquent facts of her career. In her essays, as in her translations, she concerns herself with problems of ethics and freedom. In seeking a way to deal with narrowing, ungenerous orthodoxies, she turns from the maxims of dogmatists to the inclusive assertions of art. The highest ethical values in her work are aesthetic ones; and this is a view with the most immediate, practical social and even political relevance.

"Much twaddling criticism has been spent on Carlyle's style," she wrote (*Essays,* 214), and the remark applies equally to much of the criticism spent on George Eliot's ideas of morality and of realism. Most notable is the view that there are contradictions in George Eliot's work (and mind) between realism and morality. She herself comments directly on the value of such a view:

> It is an old bias to suppose that we can delight in conceiving men as they ought to be only by shutting our eyes to what they are, & that otherwise we shall not believe in their having those elements or qualities which can make them grow towards what they ought to be. Looked at closely this notion seems to hold in it the utmost possible scepticism as to human goodness, & is an indirect assertion that society is to be saved by silliness & pretence. Everybody can see what mischief would follow if we carried this kind of willful illusion into our working of metals & our building of bridges. Among some peoples it has been held that fishes could be enticed by flattery & that a storm could be quieted by a present of tobacco. But it is now pretty well agreed in this quarter of the ⟨world⟩ globe that we are the better off for knowing better the nature of fishes & storms & acting according to that knowledge. [17]

Though the writing in this late essay has not been corrected for print, the thought is plain enough. Such misconception, distorting the power to deal with practical issues, is something George Eliot devoted much attention to during her career. What is moral and what is real are only divisible if one separates moral issues from human particulars, and this is a move against which George Eliot devoted her considerable energy and capabilities throughout a long career.

Far from being opposed in George Eliot's work, moral and practical issues are constantly joined. Order, beauty, ethical behavior, freedom: these are not "natural" but artificial results of human effort. "The selfish instincts are not subdued by the sight of buttercups, nor is integrity in the least established by that classic rural occupation, sheep washing. To make men moral, something more is requisite than to turn them out to grass" (*Essays,* 270). Like the aesthetic qualities sought and explored in George Eliot's novels, morality is an artificial, not natural result. Like art, morality is an achieved, in fact a highly achieved effect. It would not be too much to say that life itself is a form of art: an activity of shaping results that calls on the powers of the artist in every individual. She wrote in her earliest published fiction about the potential identity of life and art:

I love to watch the artist's eye, so wrapt and unworldly in its glance, scrupulously attentive to the details of his actual labour, yet keeping ever in view the idea which that labour is to fulfill. I say to myself,—this is an image of what our life should be,—a series of efforts directed to the production of a contemplated whole, just as every stroke of the artist's pencil has a purpose bearing on the conception which he retains in his mind's eye. We should all be painting our picture. (*Essays,* 18)

It is clear from everything she wrote that morality for George Eliot is not a matter of views; what is "right" or "wrong," doctrines, maxims, received truths or exploratory ones, all have limited value as guides to life, in the mixed, entangled affair of human experience. Both art and morality stand together, opposed to the falsifying prescriptive generalizations against which she constantly worked. Realism, whether in art or morality—(the two are scarcely separable)—is opposed to "falsism"[18] and her essays trace various ways in which such false approaches to moral life impede and even wither it. To subdue the selfish instincts one needs not doctrines, but surprise: some influence apart from habitual ones that arrests attention, turns it on one's own comfortable, customary belief, and modifies it with evidence of the human (or species) potential. Art has this power of surprising attention and, because of this, it is both realistic and moral. "Art is the nearest thing to life; it is a mode of extending our contact with our fellow men beyond the bounds of our personal lot" (*Essays,* 270–71). The act of seeing beyond one's limits strengthens self-knowledge; it is an act with aesthetic value and in that value is its highest moral quality. The morality of life is deeply a matter of form.

Because the problems and solutions of art are so continually evoked as models for life, a closer look at her view of aesthetic form is worthwhile. She has made that view explicit in her "Notes on Form in Art," written in 1868, while she was publishing her long poem on *The Spanish Gypsy* and preparing to write her fifth novel, *Middlemarch.* In these notes she develops the idea of the tensional quality of art. Structure, or form, depends on a balance of forces, a joint relation between unifying functions and diversifying ones. For example, in the human body, or the work of art, or most of all in a life, the differentiation of function makes possible the richest and most complex form or order, one that has the most varied capacity. But such variety must also have principles of repetition or unity, if it is to achieve shape and definition and not merely be dispersed in complexity. The highest form "is the most varied group of relations bound together in a wholeness which again has the most varied relations with all other phenomena" (*Essays*, 433). Art in life, or morality, is the result of a process involving tensional balance of forces: emotion and intellect, repetition and diversification, "diversifying thought" and "rhythmic persistence." Custom, for example, is a repetitive element; so are emotion and tradition. Innovation is a diversifying element; so are thought and individual experience. The aesthetic achievement depends on unifying these complementary impulses; so that thought and emotion become one; so that innovation and custom collaborate; so that individual experience and tradition can accommodate one another.

A syntax of their own: George Eliot on women. Because George Eliot cares for action, not talk about action, and because she distrusts "isms" of any kind as breeding grounds for intolerance, ideologues of all kinds are likely to have difficulty with her work. It should be clear from the discussion so far that George Eliot is not likely to be interested in the kind of idealized models for women that she satirizes in "Silly Novels by Lady Novelists." Her imagination extends beyond the easy fantasies of such fiction, piercing the solid facts of women's experience with an artist's conception. It can be seen from her portraits of women how important women are, and how thwarted they are. In representing the world as she found it, she refused to falsify her findings. She returns repeatedly in her essays and novels to the condition of women; in particular, to the crippling demands made and the deprivations forced upon women by constrictive conventions; to the strength of women's will or intelligence; to women's social isolation and their real claims to the wider life so often denied them; and to the real difficulties of independent achievement in the face of sexist assumptions. Her representations are radical and uncompromising, and always tuned to what is, not what ought to be.

For example, Gwendolen Harleth, in her last novel, is gradually stripped of all her trivial instruments of power, until at the end of the book she is alone, with her mother, unmarried and with no professional or marital prospects. At once intelligent and ignorant, Gwendolen has to learn her limits before she can take her place as an adult, and her task is all the more massive and threatening because she has been sold a bill of goods concerning her proper role and possibilities. She plays at reigning, but she has no real power until she first learns that she has none. At the end of the novel, the male protagonist, Daniel Deronda, has a career, a heritage and, despite its unlikeliness, a character with the power to withstand and to shape the oddities of his circumstances. Gwendolen, on the other hand, has a general, new-born will to "be better," but she is conspicuously without instruments at hand. Does this seem fair? Not at all, and George Eliot demonstrates this inequity quite plainly; but wishing it were otherwise has only led Gwendolen into worse confusion. It is Gwendolen's recognition of her actual circumstances—actual in that no magic can dismiss them—that marks the beginning of her real access to power.

By contrast, a romantic portrait of the kind offered by lady novelists in silly novels leaves the heroine with all manner of success and the reader with a lie. This heroine, described by George Eliot as belonging to the "mind-and-millinery" species, has effortless success. She reads the Scriptures in their original tongues. "Of course! Greek and Hebrew are mere play to a heroine; Sanscrit is no more than *a b c* to her; and she can talk with perfect correctness in any language except English. She is a polking polyglott, a Creuzer in crinoline. Poor men! There are so few of you who know even Hebrew. . . ."

Her eyes and her wit are both dazzling. . . . She has a superb *contralto* and a superb intellect. . . . Rakish men either bite their lips in impotent confusion at her repartees, or are touched to penitence by her reproofs. . . . The men play a very subordinate part by her side. You are consoled now and then by a hint that they have affairs, which keeps you in mind that the working-day business of the world is somehow being carried on, but ostensibly the final cause of their existence is that they may accompany the heroine on her 'starring' expedition through life. (*Essays,* 302–5)

Such an image is a cruel joke for real women in the real world, coping with real and particular circumstances. This pulp romance or soap opera kind of existence is a flight from hard circumstances and painful truths. In condemning such novels, George Eliot thus feels no scruple in her sarcasm, especially because such silly novels "rarely introduce us to any other than very lofty and fashionable society." In her portraits of Gwendolen, or of Rosamond Vincy in *Middlemarch* ("the flower of Mrs. Lemon's school"), in demonstrating the terrible pain inflicted on ignorant Hetty Sorrel in *Adam Bede,* or in demonstrating the disaster of Maggie Tulliver's not maturing, in these and in other compelling portraits, she treats women seriously by taking seriously their real circumstances. She takes others to task precisely for trivializing the important subject. At the end of a review of one novel, for example, she writes: "We care too much for the attainment of a better understanding as to women's true position, not be sorry when a writer like Miss Jewsbury only adds her voice to swell the confusion on this subject" (*Essays,* 136).

She returns in various ways to the tyranny of ignorance and weakness in women's lot. She reviews with evident approval some strong statements by Margaret Fuller and Mary Wollstonecraft "on the folly of absolute definitions of woman's nature and absolute demarcations of woman's mission"; the oppression of women, like that of any other group, has resulted in debility and feebleness both in mind and will, and such oppression is only perpetuated by fairy-tales of the sort found in sentimental and empty idealizations. She emphasizes the profound importance of such oppression for men and women alike. "Men pay a heavy price for their reluctance to encourage self-help and independent resources in women" (*Essays,* 203–5), something George Eliot and Lewes had only too thorough knowledge of with Agnes. "Let the whole field of reality be laid open to woman as well as to man, and then that which is peculiar in her mental modification, instead of being, as it is now, a source of discord and repulsion between the sexes, will be found to be a necessary complement to the truth and beauty of life" (*Essays,* 81).

Some important essays.   Of her many fine review essays, five in particular will serve to suggest her range and wit. One is her first essay for the *Westminster Review,* written just before she joined Chapman and less than three years before she began translating Feuerbach. Robert William Mackay's *Progress of the Intellect* (1850) developed the idea, one to which she was already sympathetic, "that divine revelation is not contained exclusively or preeminently in the facts and inspirations of any one age or nation, but is co-extensive with the history of human development" (*Essays,* 30). It was a custom of nineteenth-century reviewing to use the publication of a book or a group of books as an occasion for an essay on some subject of general interest. Marian's procedures are no exception, and one must always take care to distinguish between the summary of an author's argument and Marian Evans's personal view. One can tell, for example, that she feels general approval for the views expressed in the important summary of Mackay's ideas on the history of human development. He finds that this history reveals the kind of regularities or "laws" or principles for controlling experimental activity that are found in physical science but that are "still perversely ignored in our social organization, our ethics, and our religion" (31). In other words, the presence of law rather than magic in ethical and religious and social life gives humanity a basis for controlling its destiny. Even failed experiments are important means of discovery: "Every mistake, every absurdity into which poor human nature has fallen, may be looked on as an experiment of which we may reap the benefit" (31). Such a perception encourages the large tolerance in which George Eliot the novelist was so interested. Mackay's volumes encourage readers, she says, to consider the stages of human development (not necessarily progress), and in so doing to practice changing one's point of view, an activity "which resembles an expansion of one's own being" (29). Here she expresses already the interest in learning as a way to overcome limitation that was partly to draw her to Feuerbach and Spinoza.

Her essay on "Evangelical Teaching: Dr. Cumming" (*Westminster Review*, October 1855) is a masterpiece of intelligence and of controversial wit. It was this essay, apparently, that convinced Lewes of her genius. Dr. John Cumming was a leading Evangelical minister whose influence seems far to have outreached his capabilities. It is an outrage, she writes, to see the use he makes of the authority conferred on him automatically by his position. A member of Parliament may have to face rebuttal from the opposition; a lecturer may see his audience trickle out; "but the preacher is completely master of the situation: no one may hiss, no one may depart" (*Essays,* 161). If he puts imbecilities in the mouths of opponents, and misrepresents both their doctrines and his, no one may refute him.

Given a man of moderate intellect, a moral standard not higher than the average, some rhetorical affluence and great glibness of speech, what is the career in which, without the aid of birth or money, he may most easily attain power and reputation in English society? Where is that Goshen of mediocrity in which a smattering of science and learning will pass for profound instruction, where platitudes will be accepted as wisdom, bigoted narrowness as holy zeal, unctuous egoism as God-given piety? Let such a man become an evangelical preacher; he will then find it possible to reconcile small ability with great ambition.

Her translations, her novels and stories, not to mention her own young adulthood, all suggest her clear sympathy with the power of Evangelicalism, rightly directed toward and expressed in action. All the more reason to attack the evidences of Dr. Cumming's mind in his actions, most particularly his style, which, like his habit of mind, is "exuberant but not exact" (164). Actions are ideas, and ideas are acts. In Dr. Cumming's expressions the reviewer learns what his morality and credibility are made of.

Three characteristics in particular interest her. First, his "*unscrupulosity of statement*" (165). The "flagrant unveracity" she finds in his pages, shows a mental habit that "blunts not only the perception of truth, but the sense of truthfulness." He is content to establish his faith on fallacies, so that he no longer inquires "concerning a proposition whether it is attested by sufficient evidence, but whether it accords with Scripture"; such minds "do not search for facts, as such, but for facts that will bear out their doctrine." In this Dr. Cumming "is much in the same intellectual condition as that Professor of Padua, who, in order to disprove Galileo's discovery of Jupiter's satellites, urges that as there were only seven metals there could not be more than seven planets" (167). To such superstition as this, everything is twisted for the sake of a preexistent dogma, and the grotesqueness of the distortion is in proportion to the smallness of the mind doing the twisting. How can such a mind be credited when it comes to the ultimate questions of existence? "In marshalling the evidence of Christianity, Dr. Cumming directs most of his arguments against opinions that are . . . totally imaginary. . . . He is meeting a hypothesis which no one holds, and totally missing the real question" (171). Nowhere is he humble, candid, or sympathetic; "everywhere he supposes the doubter is hardened, conceited, consciously shutting his eyes to the light—a fool who is to be answered according to his folly—that is, with ready replies made up of reckless assertions, of apocryphal anecdotes, and, where other resources fail, of vituperative imputations" (173–74). The circularity of his logic, clearly demonstrated in the review, "would be an almost pathetic self-exposure, if it were not disgusting. Imbecility that is not even meek, ceases to be pitiable and becomes simply odious" (178).

The second characteristic of Dr. Cumming's teaching is its *"absence of genuine charity."* Though he professes liberality and brotherly love among Christians, it is for a narrow circle only, and "the love thus taught is the love of the *clan,* which is the correlative of antagonism to the rest of mankind. . . . Dr. Cumming's religion may demand a tribute of love, but it gives a charter to hatred; it may enjoin charity, but it fosters all uncharitableness. He recognizes men only as Christians, and Christians only "in the sense of a small minority. . . . But who that is in the slightest degree acquainted with the action of the human mind, will believe that any genuine and large charity can grow out of an exercise of love which is always to have an *arriere-pensee* of hatred? Of what quality would be the conjugal love of a husband who loved his spouse as a wife, but hated her as a woman?" (180).

The third characteristic of Dr. Cumming's writing is the *"perverted moral judgment* that everywhere reigns in them" (184). Rather than encouraging charity or forbearance or justice as motives in themselves moral, he encourages them only as they fulfill his view of the glory of God. His writings are full of this perverted morality. "The sense of alarm and haste, the anxiety for personal safety, which Dr. Cumming insists upon as the proper religious attitude, unmans the nature, and allows no thorough, calm-thinking, no truly noble, disinterested feeling" (168). All affection, discretion, courage, and charity are supplanted by "anxiety for the 'glory of God' " (187). His God is in constant opposition to human sympathies, dividing them in suspicion or even hatred, and exhorting them not to care for each other "except as they have relation to Him; He is a God, who . . . commands us to check these impulses, lest they should prevent us from thinking of His glory" (188). Worst of all, this approach to morality deflects the believer from exercise of his or her human faculties, an exercise that is more in tune with the best conceptions of divinity than all the evangelical teaching of Dr. Cumming.

"The Natural History of German Life" (*Westminster Review,* July 1856) is a review of Wilhelm von Riehl's pioneering works on cultural history. His immediate subject is the German peasantry and its relation to modern political ideas and movements. The more we inquire into the actual conditions of people, Riehl suggests, "The more thoroughly we shall be convinced that a *universal social policy has no validity except on paper,* and can never be carried into successful practice. The conditions of German society are altogether different from those of French, English, or Italian society; and to apply the same social theory to these nations indiscriminately, is about as wise" as applying "the agricultural directions in Virgil's 'Georgics' to [a] farm in the Shetland Isles" (*Essays,* 289). Political "doctrinaires" merely falsify their possibilities by reductive theorizing concerning any class of society, whether "Parisian proletairs or English factory-workers" or the German peasant. George Eliot found in Riehl a writer who not only shared her dislike for dogma but also one who could write intelligently on the actual conditions of a peasant class with which she had some familiarity and that had little connection with the romanticised "operatic peasants" found in many aesthetic treatments.

Her summary of Riehl's discussion suggests that peasantry is more a matter of mental habit than of social class. The peasant is someone who regards his customs as having the force of natural law. The way they do things, is the way it is: part of the "eternal fitness of things" as the Dodsons and Tullivers conceive it in her second novel, a book that might be considered a complementary statement treating the natural history of English life. To the peasant (as to the religious dogmatist and the political doctrinaire) his way is the right way, any other is simply wrong. Such a view makes impossible a society founded on law. "Systematic cooperation implies general conceptions," based on comparisons; but where no valid differences are allowed, no fruitful comparisons can be made (283). The bearing on people like Dr. Cumming begins to be apparent. He, too, encourages the divisive *clan* allegiance that makes general cooperation and tolerance impossible. Aristocrats are a similar case. "The inheritance of titles by younger sons is the universal custom, and custom is stronger than law"; despite any legal opposition, feudal custom prevails as much in the upper classes as in the lower.

But even such peasants are preferable to the *"Philister"* (Riehl's word), or philistine, one who "is indifferent to all social interests, all public life, as distinguished from selfish and private interests; he has no sympathy with political and social events except as they affect his own comfort and prosperity." Such characters appear frequently in George Eliot's novels, and are even discussed directly in a late essay, ostensibly written by one of her characters, Felix Holt. In his terms, a philistine is any scoundrel "whether he is a rich religious scoundrel who lies and cheats on a large scale, and will perhaps come and ask you to send him to Parliament, or a poor pocket-picking scoundrel, who will steal your loose pence while you are listening round the platform" (*Essays,* 419). Such a person is incapable of perceiving that what injures society injures him, what benefits it benefits him; he acknowledges only the service it can do him, having none of the civilized sense "of a common interest in preventing injury." In stating Riehl's opinions, Marian Evans reminds us, she is not quoting Riehl so much "as interpreting and illustrating him" (287). This essay has considerable relevance for George Eliot's portraits of rural people in her first two novels.

Her essay on "Worldliness and Other-Worldliness: The Poet Young" (*Westminster Review,* January 1857), like her essay on Dr. Cumming, explores the implications of a style and a life that she knew well and that had generated adolescent enthusiasm. In the case of the eighteenth-century poet Young, the telling feature of his work is its flight into abstraction, and she summarizes her case as follows: "The sum of our comparison is this—In Young we have the type of that deficient human sympathy, that impiety towards the present and the visible, which flies for its motives, its sanctities, and its religion, to the remote, the vague, and the unknown: in Cowper [by contrast] we have the type of that genuine love which cherishes things in proportion to their nearness, and feels its reverence grow in proportion to the intimacy of its knowledge" (*Essays,* 385). She quotes the following example from Young: "Far beneath/A soul immortal is a mortal joy," and comments, "Young could utter this falsity without detecting it, because, when he spoke of 'mortal joys,' he rarely had in his mind any object to which he could attach sacredness. He was thinking of bishoprics and benefices, of smiling monarchs, patronizing prime ministers, and a 'much indebted muse.' Of anything between these and eternal bliss, he was but rarely and moderately conscious" (386). Her treatment justifies some quotation because her own writing so clearly presages the novelist.

For example she presents his characteristic habit of dualism and antithesis (a familiar eighteenth-century poetic and stylistic device) as follows:

"Earth" means lords and levees, duchesses and Dalilahs, South-Sea dreams and illegal percentage; and the only things distinctly preferable to these are, eternity and the stars. Deprive Young of this antithesis, and more than half

his eloquence would be shriveled up. Place him on a breezy common, where
the furze is in its golden bloom, where children are playing, and horses are
standing in the sunshine with fondling necks, and he would have nothing to
say. (368–69)

She links his adherence to abstractions with a *"want of genuine emo-*
tion," in other words an incapacity to imagine actual, individual life.
"Now, emotion links itself with particulars, and only in a faint and
secondary manner with abstractions. . . . Generalities apart from
particulars . . . are the refuge at once of deficient intellectual activity
and deficient feeling" (371). Another symptom of "Young's deficiency in moral, i.e., in sympathetic emotion, is his unintermitting
habit of pedagogic moralizing" (379).

Young's problem, as she presents it, is at least partly his belief in
his own, personal immortality. "Young has no conception of religion
as anything else than egoism turned heaven-ward; and he does not
merely imply this, he insists on it. Religion, he tells us, in argumen-
tative passages too long to quote, is 'ambition, pleasure, and the love
of gain', directed towards the joys of the future life instead of the present. And his ethics correspond to his religion" (378). Such views are
perfectly in keeping with a life spent sniffing about after preferment.
"After being a hanger-on of the profligate Duke of Wharton, after
aiming in vain at a parliamentary career, and angling for pensions and
preferment with fulsome dedications and fustian odes, he is a little
disgusted with his imperfect success, and has determined to retire
from the general mendicancy business to a particular branch; in other
words, he has determined on that renunciation of the world implied
in 'taking orders', with the prospect of a good living and an advanta-
geous matrimonial connection" (337). A man so alive to his personal
interests, so abstract in his moralizing, so personally grasping and
publicly obsequious, does not live altogether in the real world of political activity, where one's commitment to honesty generally is
made, not because one expects to live "in another world, but because,
having felt the pain of injustice and dishonesty" in this, one shrinks
from inflicting the same pain on others (373). In this essay we find
the emphasis on sympathy, the attention to particular existence so evident in the novelist George Eliot, who was being born at almost this
time in the first "Scene" of clerical life, published in the year following this essay on the poet Young.

"The Influence of Rationalism" (*Fortnightly Review*, 15 May 1865), appeared seven years after George Eliot began publishing fiction, and while she was writing *Felix Holt*. A review of W. E. H. Lecky's two-volume history of European rationalism, the essay expresses especially eloquently some of her long-standing ideas concerning the competition of reasonableness against superstition, and concerning the mutually informative relationship between individuals and the cultural matrix in which they find themselves. Since Lecky does not define rationalism, she does, emphasizing (as Lecky does not) the importance of science in contributing to the gradual rejection of the miraculous and reduction of phenomena to spheres of established law. She writes:

The great conception of universal regular sequence, without partiality and without caprice—the conception which is the most potent force at work in the modification of our faith, and of the practical form given to our sentiments—could only grow out of that patient watching of external fact and that silencing of preconceived notions, which are urged upon the mind by the problems of physical science. (413)

This is far from saying that there is a science of social life; such a notion does not appear in her work at all. What it does say, however, is that the habits of science—patience, and silencing of preconceptions—have made possible the perception of regularities in human experience that operate on individual lives despite wishing, and that must be consulted in making choices and pursuing action. Such conditions act on the mind like a kind of "external Reason. . . . No seances at a guinea a head for the sake of being pinched by 'Mary Jane' can annihilate railways, steamships, and electric telegraphs. . . . These things are part of the external Reason to which internal silliness has inevitably to accommodate itself" (402). The fact that restraints have been placed on superstition and cruelty at all is partly due to the pressure of such conditions, that is, to the diffuse influence of individual lives working in countless corners of the human universe. This sum of conditions, if perceived, quiets the grasping ego with a vastness that no mind can compass and that thus promotes collaboration and cooperation instead of intolerance and persecution.

Besides reflecting her exuberant wit, George Eliot's essays and translations offer her readers the most infallible guide to her interests, apart from the novels: among them her interests in the links, for better or worse, between individual and collective life through the powers of consciousness and language; in the spirit of tolerance entailed by this fundamental condition; in the artificiality of culture as distinct from nature and in culture's profound freedoms; in the inseparability of ideas and things; and in the excitement and opportunity as well as the responsibility of knowledge. These are among the concerns evident in her early career that remain in her fiction as guiding, structuring intuitions.

Chapter Three

Common Ground: *Scenes of Clerical Life, Adam Bede, The Mill on the Floss*

Human life as George Eliot presents it in her fiction is fundamentally independent of nature. In her work what is specifically human belongs exclusively to the realm of culture and this means that culture, because it is social, is automatically moral because it automatically involves dealings among people, either directly through personal contact or indirectly through tradition. "Amiable impulses without intellect, man may have in common with dogs and horses; but morality, which is specifically human, is dependent on the regulation of feeling by intellect. All human beings who can be said to be in any degree moral have their impulses guided, not indeed always by their own intellect, but by the intellect of human beings who have gone before them, and created traditions and associations which have taken the rank of laws."[1] According to George Eliot, human beings share in common a debt to tradition so extensive that it is nearly impossible to measure. The history that has become embedded in the accumulated artifacts of civilization, from its simplest tools to its languages and institutions, has become a second nature to human beings, an artificial environment that is inescapable, that does not depend upon any larger natural or cosmic system of explanation, and that is the basis for all individual achievement.

The realm of culture as George Eliot conceives it is full of conflicting claims, diverse possibilities, and a bewildering array of evidence that can make it seem a hopeless wilderness to the individual looking for a reliable guide to choice, especially the important choice of vocation. But the confusion of culture is symptomatic of its greatest benefit, its freedom from any single system of explanation. When life is such a tangled affair it is optimistic "cant" to pretend it has an easily traceable plan; but precisely *because* conditions are so diverse, what an individual can do is also diverse. There are alternatives to every choice and to every result, and thus it matters considerably what an individual does. Because people share a common ground in culture, each depending on it heavily and unconsciously, individual action inevitably modifies circumstances in ways that reach far beyond intention with effects that are incalculably diffusive. The ordinary, habitual acts in her view are the most profoundly important because, taken cumulatively, they are what make or break personal ambition, or even a collective ideal.

In George Eliot's presentation of it, culture is "common" in two senses: it is general, common to all; and it is ordinary, commonplace rather than exotic or extreme. In chapter 17 of *Adam Bede* the narrator presents a well-known expression of interest in common life:

> Certainly I could, if I held it the highest vocation of the novelist to represent things as they never have been and never will be . . . refashion life and character entirely after my own liking. . . . Perhaps you will say, "Do improve on the facts a little, then; make them more accordant with those correct views which it is our privilege to possess. The world is not just what we like; do touch it up with a tasteful pencil, and make believe it is not quite such a mixed entangled affair."

The narrative voice, however, represents a different sensibility from the one with "correct" views; it is one that takes people "as they are," trying neither to "straighten their noses, nor brighten their wit, nor rectify their dispositions. . . . It is so needful we should remember their existence, else we may happen to leave them quite out of our religion and philosophy, and frame lofty theories which only fit a world of extremes."[2] This deliberately constructed narrative consciousness is a sensibility that has little patience for people with "correct" views, and that includes all life without regard to its correctness. In a world where there are so many conflicting versions of correctness, so the implication goes, being "correct," like being "right" or "wrong," is a fantasy applicable to a world that never was and never will be; it does not belong in the actual world where one must live and make difficult choices.

The narrator in this passage typically presents itself in dialogue; not as one voice with a single correct view, but as several voices with competing views, and including even some irony at the expense of the reader. This narrative voice is conspicuously inclusive, and resistant to judgmental distinctions of the sort that are used to justify exclusiveness of all kinds. The line between vice and virtue, as George Eliot says in an essay, "so far from being a necessary safeguard to morality, is itself an immoral fiction."³ Such judgmental distinctions, which are nearly always reversible, segregate the common ground whereas the drift in George Eliot's novels consistently moves against the vulgarity of exclusiveness. Her fiction shows the personal and collective impoverishment that follows when an individual's consciousness of identity depends on negative, exclusive definition; such a person cannot tolerate or deal with the inevitable conflict and ambiguity of human culture.

Her sense of the common ground is quite distinct, however, from one usage. When we think of what is "general" or "common" we may think in terms of compromise, that is, in terms of common denominators that depreciate the unique characteristics of things in favor of the characteristics they share with other things. George Eliot's conception of the common ground, on the other hand, has little to do with common denominators. What people have in common are their differences. She looks for the distinctive feature, the particular arrangement, not for features of a species or generic arrangements. While everyone shares a common ground in culture, culture does not exist as an abstraction, any more than individuals do. Culture exists only in the sum of the diverse array of particulars, uniquely arranged and selected in each individual case. The conditions of a milkmaid are not those of a London editor. Though the inescapable *fact* of culture is the same for both in their customs and languages and most basic conceptions, they may observe different customs, speak different languages, and differ in even the most basic conceptions. Such is the realm of culture, and in such a realm there can be no final truth about good and evil. What is a good for one person is often an evil for another; valid ideas can lose influence while tendencies that should be resisted can be mistaken for inevitable laws; improvements are relative and involve both creation and displacement. The passage from her essay on *Antigone* cited in chapter 2 is worth repeating for its pertinence here.

We shall never be able to attain a great right without also doing a great wrong. . . . Preach against false doctrines, you disturb feeble minds and send them adrift on a sea of doubt; make a new road, and you annihilate vested interests; cultivate a new region of the earth, and you exterminate a race of men. Wherever the strength of man's intellect, or moral sense, or affection brings him into opposition with the rule which society has sanctioned, *there* is renewed the conflict between Antigone and Creon; such a man must not only dare to be right, he must also dare to be wrong—to shake faith, to wound friendship, perhaps, to hem in his own powers.[4]

If there were a clear right and wrong, based on a single dispensation of human affairs, there would be no need for daring to be wrong. All action could be evaluated according to the law; there could be no conflict of valid claims because all truly valid claims would be consistent with the true law and thus with each other. Such a world would be less confusing than the entangled world of culture, and less free. The principle of individuation so important in George Eliot's work produces the richness and variety of culture and, inevitably at the same time, produces conflict. There is no abstraction like "culture" or "society" to resolve them, but only the sum of particulars to which those terms loosely refer.

The absence in her work of a single dispensation, either divine or natural, does not deprive individuals of coherence and meaning, but only of absolute coherence and meaning. What people find in culture is full of meaning and coherence because it is the result of purpose and willed action; but the meanings and coherences are plural and conflicting, requiring new purpose and willed action from each individual. "All actions men put a bit of thought into are ideas," says a character in her last novel, "say, sowing seed, or making a canoe, or baking clay; and such ideas as these work themselves into life and go on growing with it."[5] Unlike the objects of nature, the objects of culture submit to no single universal idea, but are themselves embodied ideas. Culture may have no inherent purpose but each particular in culture is itself an achieved purpose. The particulars of culture are embodiments of ideas; they are results or residues of purposive action however far the outcome may be from the original intention. When George Eliot speaks in her essays of society as "incarnate history," or when she says that "even our sentiments are organised traditions; and a large part of our actions gather all their justification, all their attraction and aroma, from the memory of the life lived, of the actions done, before we were born," she employs this conception of culture-as-incarnation that is so central to her work.[6] It is a conception sufficiently unfamiliar to have generated a vast amount of misreading of her work, the chief difficulty being that she insists on the *concreteness* of what is general. What we share is culture, but culture is only available in particular forms, each unique, and each absolute in the sense that it absolutely exists and cannot be altered by wishes or magic. Tradition only exists in such incarnations of human effort, only embodied and particular in this or that person, event, artifact, institution.

The sum of such particulars is culture, or, what in the review of Lecky she calls "external Reason"—something that refers not to some transcendent reasoner, but to the collective effect of human reason as it is expressed in these incarnations. For example, to the extent that modern people avoid superstition and cruelty, it

is not because they possess a cultivated Reason, but because they are pressed upon and held up by what we may call an external Reason—the sum of conditions resulting from the laws of material growth, from changes produced by great historical collisions shattering the structures of ages and making new highways for events and ideas, and from the activities of higher minds no longer existing merely as opinion and teaching, but as institutions and organisations with which the interests, the affections, and the habits of the multitude are inextricably interwoven.

Parliaments and prayer books, the increase of population and the behavior of foreign nations, paintings and personalities, railways and even the simplest tools of domestic life are all "part of the external Reason to which internal silliness has inevitably to accommodate itself."[7] This sum of achieved results is the common ground; it has no inherent purpose of its own, but only the sum of achieved and conflicting purposes of individuals, and each incarnation itself is both the end of an artificial process and the potential beginning of others. George Eliot is always alert to the diffusive influence of individual action reacting in this highly modifiable environment.

The inconsistent diversity of the cultural ground makes it permanently resistant to finality and to absolutes, both of which she treats as other names "for bewilderment and defeat."[8] Conflict is inevitable and a sign of cultural health, not, as D. R. Carroll suggests, a sign that "the social organism has broken down."[9] The power to sustain controlled conflict is one of the highest social achievements. It is power that belongs most notably to Mordecai in her last novel, *Daniel Deronda* (592), whose "resistant" energy acts in opposition to the "resistant" disbelief of those who hear him—a mutual resistance that benefits both sides and that requires no resolution. Perhaps the real sign of disorder in her novels is the inability to gain strength from such collisions and the tendency either to withdraw from them, as some characters do, into a limbo of irresolution that produces nothing, or to become dogmatic and absolute, forgetting the relative validity of all claims. Human circumstances being what they are in George Eliot's fiction—particular but inconsistent, determinate but not deterministic—the challenge to her characters is how to be effective without being absolute, how to be flexible without being weak. In the inherited confusions of culture there is no secure, constant disposition for motive, so one cannot rely on "the way things are" to justify action or guide choice; and because the conditions of culture are determinate, incarnate, always particular, one cannot simply do "as one likes" because the sheer existence of the "external Reason" qualifies opportunity and power.

George Eliot's answer to these dilemmas is a double imperative of resignation and activity. Instead of doing as one likes, or doing as one must, it is possible to combine these two motives to sustain limited but actual achievement. "I have not given up doing as I like," says Will Ladislaw in *Middlemarch,* "but I can very seldom do it."[10] If a life of constant pleasure and satisfaction is impossible, the alternative is not merely hardship and self-suppression, but rather pleasure conceived as part of a unified labor, a benefit of exertion rather than a flight from it. More than once she cites with approval Comte's sentence, "Our true destiny is composed of resignation and activity."[11] The free individual accepts given circumstances as the necessary preliminary to action, not as a dismal foreclosure of it. Whenever she speaks of "resignation" or of the "inevitable" she speaks of half of a double imperative that requires a sort of double vision of circumstances as they are and circumstances as they might be. The one rule that "need never be changed, however often the chapter of more special rules may have to be re-written" is the imperative "never to beat and bruise one's wings against the inevitable but to throw the whole force of one's soul towards the achievement of some possible better" (*Letters,* 4:499). A clear-eyed acceptance of what cannot be changed is the essential prerequisite of achievement, and with that resignation or acceptance comes the perception of those possibilities that are so evident in all her novels. The silent power of possibilities, the power of freedom, is evident in the alternatives continually forced upon characters by the nature of cultural circumstances. One of the brilliant accomplishments of her fiction is her representation of the slow processes by which trivial moments and choices compound themselves, making iron habits that produce either failure and second-rateness, or success and excellence.

The model of success appears very early in George Eliot's work, many years before she started writing fiction, in the short essay written for the Coventry *Herald and Observer* entitled "How to Avoid Disappointment." Here the model for successful action is the artist, someone who shapes a given material for a particular end. The passage, also cited above in chapter 2 ("The morality of art"), is important enough to be repeated here:

I love to watch the artist's eye, so wrapt and unworldly in its glance, scrupulously attentive to the details of his actual labour, yet keeping ever in view the idea which that labour is to fulfil. I say to myself,—this is the image of what our life should be,—a series of efforts directed to the production of a contemplated whole, just as every stroke of the artist's pencil has a purpose bearing on the conception which he retains in his mind's eye. We should all be painting our picture. . . . We should all have a purpose in life as perfectly recognized and definite as the painter's idea of his subject.

Such purpose is something one lives with, but not for; it is experimental, always retaining its provisional nature; it is determining yet chosen for some purpose more stable than immediate or trivial satisfactions of the kind sought by the man of the world, or the man of public spirit.

"Indisputably," says your man of the world, "I have never for a moment swerved from the determination to make myself rich and respectable. I chose my wife with that object; I send my sons to the University, I give dinners, I go to balls, I go to Church,—all that I may be 'respectable.' Am I not a man of purpose?" Then there is the man of public spirit, who has devoted his life to some pet project, which is to be the grand catholicon for all the diseases of society. He has travelled, he has lectured, he has canvassed, he has moved heaven and earth, has become the victim of a fixed idea, and died disappointed. Doubtless, such men as these have a distinct purpose in life, but they are not the men of whom my artist reminds me—who seem to me to be painting a picture.

The reliable purpose is one with a value independent of "any individual, any specific form": "something which, while it dwells in these, has an existence beyond them . . . so that if the individual pass away, if the object be frustrated, his love and his labour are not essentially disappointed."[12] The characters who succeed in their aims are those who treat their circumstances as the artist treats his or her material—material to be shaped by a vision that is unique and personal and yet, by virtue of its inward and outward roots in tradition and culture, part of the common ground.

George Eliot's first stories and novels represent single communities composed of individuals who take their common estate for granted, as if it were natural like rocks and stones and trees. The plots concern ways in which such individuals learn, usually through some trauma in their midst, that the customs and views sustaining them cannot be taken for granted; that they are achieved results to which there are alternatives, rather than absolutes belonging to the eternal fitness of things. Each story shows how diffusive is an individual's influence, how the most powerful influence is often the most indirect, and how an indirect series of developments can transform the ecology of an entire community. Each story focuses on individual characters and on the question whether their lives will be dispersed among hindrances or concentrated in recognizable deeds.

Scenes of Clerical Life

Although George Eliot may have considered writing fiction while in her twenties, it was many years later that she published the three stories called *Scenes of Clerical Life* that started her on her career as a novelist. Published in *Blackwood's Magazine* (1857–58) they concern three different moments in the life of Milby parish; each uses a foreground story as a focus for the larger system of relationships making up the community. The difficult task George Eliot sets for herself from the first is that of showing the silent, invisible actions and reactions among individuals in a group. Her technique in each case is to use a trauma of confidence to suggest an awakening, and an attending recognition that is powerful, without being melodramatic.

"The Sad Fortunes of Amos Barton" concerns the parson, Amos Barton, and the tendency to self-absorption and smugness that he seems to share with his parishioners and neighbors. He is "one of those men who have a decided will and opinion of their own; he held himself bolt upright, and had no self-distrust. He would march very determinedly along the road he thought best; but then it was wonderfully easy to convince him which *was* the best road."[13] His neighbor,

Mrs. Patten, maintains her easy sense of superiority by condescending to her neighbors, parson, and relatives. She loves her money as she used to love her husband, and now looks forward mainly to disappointing her niece in her will. "Quiescence in an easy-chair, under the sense of compound interest perpetually accumulating, has long seemed an ample function to her, and she does her malevolence gently" (pp. 6–7; ch. 1). Though the intentions of these ordinary folk are not evil, though their influence is gentle, nevertheless "malevolence" is not too strong a word. This is most clearly the case for Amos's wife, Milly Barton, who tries to cope with the grinding poverty forced by the system of church livings upon those who do most of its actual parish work, and to cope in addition with the strains of a large household and two self-absorbed individuals who give her orders. Amos occupies himself with seeking advancement, strains his household with foolish and expensive ambitions; he courts the favor of a "countess" of uncertain origins whom he eventually adds to an already overburdened household, putting still more stress on his uncomplaining, patient, exhausted wife. He takes her for granted in the same way his neighbors take each other for granted, comforted by his clear sense of his own rectitude. An angry housemaid finally delivers the "countess" of her illusion that she is welcome, and so delivers the Bartons from her, but not soon enough for Milly, who has worn her health to a point where she is too weak to survive another childbirth. What awakens Amos and the others from moral slumber is not persuasion, or imaginative grasp, but the one event that can convey the absolute importance of cherishing life. Death is the great economist. Even the middling, honest property owner of Milby understands that.

George Eliot's narrator shows how the entire community is implicated in the disaster to Milly, one of its more worthy members. Their little omissions and minimal generosities, like Amos's, have contributed their long-pending influence. Milly dies of a neglect that has immediate and also more general causes. Mrs. Patten's ambition to disappoint her heirs is a life-chilling, malevolent influence that creates an atmosphere, a context of possibility for the omissions and smugness of Amos. His omissions flourish in context of hers and others so evidently like her. The surprise of death (compare the surprise of art) awakens Amos and his parishioners briefly from their illusions of supremacy, as the countess had been forced to do in facing the end of her more provisional tenure. As Amos follows Milly's coffin with a renewed respect for her worth, his parishioners, watching his pale haggardness, at least momentarily abandon their former careless contempt for him and assume a more "respectful pity."

"Mr. Gilfil's Love Story" concerns a single aristocratic family of Milby, that of Sir Christopher Cheverel and his elegant lady. George Eliot deftly portrays the vulgarity of exclusiveness in the British aristocracy, especially in their condescending kindness to Caterina (also called Tina), an Italian orphan whom they adopt in her childhood as a protégée but not as a daughter, that is, included without being included. They take her to cheer their manor, and to train her (Sir Christopher continues to call her his "little monkey"), "but neither he nor Lady Cheverel had any idea of adopting her as their daughter, and giving her their own rank in life. They were much too English and aristocratic to think of anything so romantic. No! The child would be brought up at Cheverel Manor as a protégée, to be ultimately useful, perhaps, in sorting worsteds, keeping accounts, reading aloud, and otherwise supplying the place of spectacles when her ladyship's eyes should wax dim" (p. 112; ch. 3). She is protected, trotted out to sing for guests, but it is always tacitly understood that her place is theirs to give or withhold. Clearly the thought that Tina might develop a life and hopes of her own never crosses their minds, so easily do they dismiss her as not one of their kind. Tina's sufferings as a consequence of their neglect, and the Cheverels' complete ignorance of the misery they underwrite, is the burden of this subtle story.

Mr. Gilfil's love for Caterina remains on the sidelines of the central story, a tactic George Eliot uses throughout her career to demonstrate the spreading influence of individual actions on lives near them. For the narrator, Mr. Gilfil's love for Caterina is ancient history, part of a far gone time that explains the character of the man in old age when he has long been a widower. "Many an irritating fault, many an unlovely oddity, has come of hard sorrow," and Gilfil's quirks are no exception. As he himself once told Tina, "we are always doing each other injustice, and thinking better or worse of each other than we deserve, because we only hear and see separate words and actions. We don't see each other's whole nature" (p. 197; ch. 19). Caterina's story demonstrates the full implications of this truth.

While her patrons assume that Caterina will marry Maynard Gilfil, assuming likewise that she must be of the same mind, Caterina has quite another idea. Cheverel's nephew, Anthony, engages her heart, pledges his, and then jilts her for a wealthier woman—circumstances to which the Cheverels are blinded by their own attitude toward their little monkey. Tina's response to such betrayal is a murderous reflex that only fails of its object because Anthony dies (appropriately) of a bad heart. When she disappears, driven away in shock by conflicting emotions of grief and self-hatred, her guardian finally learns the truth and, thus, his responsibility for the long-developing disaster. "God help me!" says Sir Christopher, "I thought I saw everything, and was stone-blind all the while" (p. 187; ch. 18). At this stroke he discovers the train of causes that has been obvious to readers; he has given her a home without in the least expecting her to feel completely at home there. The one thing missing from his complacent condescension to Tina is a sense that they share a common human ground and hence an essential human equality. Although they mean well, the Cheverels' class bigotry is a streak of vulgarity that always belies their elegance and prevents them from accomplishing the benign results they actually intend. Caterina survives to marry Maynard, but she does not survive long, and the shortness of her life is directly linked, clearly and despite the indirectness of causalities, to the long neglect of her protectors.

This second "Scene" gives us a glimpse of the structural sophistication of George Eliot's later work and of the narrator's important role in it. Caterina's story is framed by others, those of Maynard Gilfil, of her parents, and of France during the Revolution. These stories, introduced by the narrator, reinforce the sense of connection between events separated in time and space that is one mark of George Eliot's fiction. The hopeless story of Caterina's Italian parents, contrasting in every way with the good luck and silky comfort of the Cheverels' pampered existence, testifies further to the power of omission. Lady Cheverel feels sorry for them, and so "adopts" Caterina, flattering herself that it is enough to feel sorry. The eventual results of this complacency are indirect and circuitous but inexorable; and they suggest plainly that the system that oppressed Caterina's parents abroad is the same as the one that eventually takes its toll on her.

The narrator, in addition, enlarges the reference of this humble tale in another more surprising direction, the political. This kind of move is always in the background of George Eliot's fiction, and explicit in all her novels after the second: for example, the politics of Renaissance Florence (*Romola*), the English Reform movement (*Felix Holt, the Radical*), the politics of class, and of a locale relative to a wider national or international scene (*Middlemarch, Daniel Deronda*). In "Mr. Gilfil's

Love Story" the particular political reference is to the French Revolution. "The last chapter has given the discerning reader sufficient insight into the state of things at Cheverel Manor in the summer of
1788. In that summer, we know, the great nation of France was agi-
tated by conflicting thoughts and passions, which were but the beginning of great sorrows. And in our Caterina's little breast, too,
there were terrible struggles" (p. 107; ch. 3). This linkage between
great things and small is not arbitrary as it may seem (although the
necessity to accomplish broad connections in short space suggests one
good reason that George Eliot turned to the longer form of the
novel). The issues at stake in the French Revolution between the citizens of France and the aristocracy have immediate relevance to those
at stake in the mutual incomprehension between Caterina and her
guardians at Cheverel Manor. Both in France and at Cheverel Manor
the guardianship is inadequate, in both cases the sequence of events
concerns the struggle of hopelessness against the hard iron of circumstance, in both cases the consequences are violence and disorder.
These analogies suggest the political consequences of the ordinary
capillary action in society whereby the failure of one person or group
has broad influence re-creating or redirecting a common tradition by
accumulated daily acts. The responsibility for political circumstances
belongs not only to members of Parliament, but also to a Lady Cheverel in her well-meaning complacent ease.

"Janet's Repentance" represents Milby during the advent of Evangelicalism. Milbyans as usual regard their town as the center of the
universe and imagine that "life must be a dull affair for that large
portion of mankind who were necessarily shut out from an acquaintance with Milby families, and that it must be an advantage to London and Liverpool that Milby gentlemen occasionally visited those
places on business" (p. 223; ch. 2). This easy-going complacency provides the necessary context for the factional intensity of religious parties within Milby, particularly of the lawyer Robert Dempster, who
believes in the essential correctness of his views and, consequently in
the total incorrectness of any differing views. The events concern his
directing of his alcoholic animosities, both in a public offensive
against the Evangelical minister Edgar Tryan, and in a private offensive against his wife, whom he beats and terrorizes. Dempster makes
each of them targets for various cowardly humiliations and harrass-
ments. The story opens with Dempster's emphatic negative—
"No!"—an emblem of the community's central problem. His

strength lies in his negations, as does the strength of a community that, as a whole, regards itself as an exclusive eminence from which some businessmen occasionally depart for such inferior places as Liverpool or London.

Robert Dempster and Edgar Tryan differ widely in their awareness of common cause with other human beings. Dempster, in a better, gentler youth shown through flashbacks, has declined unopposed into a violent and brutal man with respect for nothing but his own will; even his occupation as a lawyer suggests his fundamentally combative posture toward others. Tryan, by contrast, brings to Milby the leavening influence of Evangelicalism, a religious movement that, despite its mixed effects, fosters conceptions essential to social cooperation and to individual vocation. George Eliot's fictional treatment of this movement, like her essay on Dr. Cumming, leaves no doubt of its mixed effect; nevertheless, Evangelicalism introduces an idea not unlike that of the artist's described above. Evangelicalism

had brought into palpable existence and operation in Milby society that idea of duty, that recognition of something to be lived for beyond the mere satisfaction of self, which is to the moral life what the addition of a great central ganglion is to animal life. No man can begin to mould himself on a faith or an idea without rising to a higher order of experience: a principle of subordination, of self-mastery, has been introduced into his nature; he is no longer a mere bundle of impressions, desires and impulses. (p. 282; ch. 10)

The alarm felt in Milby over this invasive influence in their drawing rooms and among the well-clad, corresponds to Milby's aesthetic and moral awakening through the discovery of a difference and, with that discovery, a dawning recognition of the vast sum of existence and influence extending beyond their small boundaries, a recognition of the wider life in which they are just one part.[14]

The story follows the pervasive influence of Tryan's ministry in the community and even into Dempster's family. Tryan's early death is linked to the solitary labor, long hours, and persecution that drain his energy and deepen the consumption already upon him before he appears in Milby. "It is apt to be so in this life, I think. While we are coldly discussing a man's career, sneering at his mistakes, blaming his rashness, and labelling his opinions—'Evangelical and narrow,' or 'Latitudinarian and Pantheistic,' or 'Anglican and supercilious' that man, in his solitude, is perhaps shedding hot tears because his sacrifice is a hard one, because strength and patience are failing him to speak the difficult word, and do the difficult deed" (p. 274; ch. 8). Milby changes its mind about Tryan too late to spare him the ultimate expense. His death, anticipated and accepted by him, contrasts with Dempster's death in an alcoholic delirium. Exactly as he did in his marriage and in his community, Dempster dies without ever "coming to himself" (p. 350; ch. 24), and without ever knowing those around him or being conscious of his mortality. Tryan makes his sacrifice consciously and for a purpose.

These deaths, important as they are, only frame the story of Janet Dempster's crisis, one that is a "type" of death: one of those moments "when we are cut off abruptly from the life we have known, when we can no longer expect tomorrow to resemble yesterday, and find ourselves by some sudden shock on the confines of the unknown" (p. 306; ch. 15). When Janet, also an alcoholic, finds herself shut out of her own house by her drunken husband in the middle of a cold night, the radical experience forces her to find alternatives. As she gradually, painfully leaves behind an old life and begins a new one, learning to avoid alcohol and suicide with the help of her old enemy Rev. Tryan, Janet makes the transition from the antisocial habits of her husband to the life-supporting habits she learns from Tryan and from other friendships. Her confessions of despair and confusion to Tryan are gestures with special value here and elsewhere in George Eliot's fiction because they represent that mutual acknowledgment of trust between individuals upon which culture rests. After his death Janet does not "feel that he was quite gone from her; the unseen world lay so very near her": a world of human feeling that survives material death and surrounds her with "the presence of unseen witnesses" (p. 376; ch. 28).

In *Scenes of Clerical Life* two features, the role of nature and the role of the narrator, warrant special mention because they have general importance in her work. In these stories and in the first two novels especially, George Eliot uses natural settings to comment on human ones. Her nature is conspicuously indifferent to man, its beauty and its coldness alike insensible to human feeling. In "Amos Barton" the community is represented by the separate domestic circle that opens the story, savoring the snug warmth of its own privacy and superiority. "While it is freezing with February bitterness outside," the Hackits take tea with Mrs. Patten and Mr. Pilgrim, and comfortably discuss their neighbors as if they were part of the natural elements, to be shut out like the winter cold, rather than part of a common human portion that they together have made and sustained. Here, as in "Gilfil" and "Janet," the cold of the elements and the cold of the grave match the mortal chill at the heart of a community that takes its mutual bonds for granted, treating fellow human beings as something to guard against or exclude, like bad weather. The garden at Cheverel Manor, an emblem of the owners' power and of their easy assumption that their ways are "natural," has a brilliant beauty that only intensifies Caterina's sorrow and "feeling of isolation" (p. 101; ch. 2). In "Janet" the heroine learns what it means to be alone in nature, on the night her husband locks her out in the street. "There would have been dead silence in Orchard Street but for the whistling of the wind and the swirling of the March dust on the pavement. Thick clouds covered the sky; every door was closed; every window was dark. No ray of light fell on the tall white figure that stood in lonely misery on the doorstep; no eye rested on Janet as she sank down on the cold stone, and looked into the dismal night. She seemed to be looking on her own blank future" (p. 306; ch. 14). The natural world is dark and cold, and associated with threats of death and thoughts of suicide. The coldness of the natural setting is a constant reminder that social and moral warmth is artificial, not natural. "The selfish instincts are not subdued by the sight of buttercups," she wrote in her essay on Riehl and thinking perhaps of the Romantic poets, "nor is integrity in the least established by that classic rural occupation, sheep-washing. To make men moral, something more is requisite than to turn them out to grass."[15] The measure of human achievement is the distance it travels from unself-conscious nature.

The second feature, the narrating voice, is crucial to George Eliot's achievement and is one of her most celebrated effects. "Is there not a pathos in their very insignificance—in our comparison of their dim and narrow existence with the glorious possibilities of that human nature which they share?" ("Amos Barton," p. 42, ch. 5). A comment like this, together with the shifts in plot focus from one snug parlor to another, reinforces the reader's awareness of the common ground ignored so often by characters. Where Milbyans may mistake their views for "natural" ones, the narrator makes that course impossible for readers, who are continually aware of the presence of alternatives and of a wider world of information and experience than that available to ordinary Milby consciousness. This narrator is sometimes associated with the author, and sometimes not, but it is never an accidental effect, or a spontaneous overflow on the part of George Eliot. Her narrative voice is a deliberate achievement, and one closely resembling that of the fictional artist she described in her first publication. In that series she declares her intention (fictionalized as that of an editor) to present to her readers the image of a mind: a particular mind belonging to a late friend, one McCarthy, whose mind has properties much like those of the artist she describes in the next installment. "His ideal was . . . a beautiful shadow which was ever floating before him, importunately presenting itself as a twin object with all realities."[16] In her novels this "shadow" is the narrative consciousness, one that is not always an individual one. Just as the artist's guiding idea or the Evangelical idea of duty in Milby guides action, so does McCarthy's ideal guide him; and for this the young George Eliot proposes to present the "image of his mind." It is such a consciousness— one aware of wider possibilities, yet restrained and particular about the details of behavior and circumstance—that develops its full wings in her novels, and accompanies the reader from first to last, enforcing a continuous vision of possibilities where characters tend to see only a repetitive round of interest. This narrator, one could even say, represents that self-awareness in the human species that Feuerbach identifies as consciousness (see above, chapter 2).

Adam Bede

George Eliot originally planned a fourth "Scene," but her subject would "not come under the limitations of the title 'Clerical Life,'" as she wrote to her publisher, so she "inclined to take a large canvas for it, and write a novel" (Letters, 2:381). "It will be a country story— full of the breath of cows and the scent of hay" (2:387). Adam Bede (1859) traces in six books six phases in the community of Hayslope, a fictional rural community rooted in custom which change threatens and alters. Book 1 introduces the separate households and separate ways of the main characters. Adam Bede is a carpenter like his father and lives with his brother Seth in the cottage where they grew up, under the care of their querulous mother Lisbeth. The death of Adam's father early in the book makes way for changes in Adam's life, changes that in his mind include the blooming Hetty Sorrel, niece of the Poysers. The Poyser household at Hall farm, compared with the plain, even constricted ways of the Bede cottage, is full of vitality, with its dairy, orchards, meadows, and children. The Poysers, in turn, are tenants of Squire Donnithorne, grandfather of young Arthur, who will soon come of age and become master in Hayslope. Arthur lives with his grandfather at the Hall, a hereditary establishment for a hereditary landlord. The small but genteel household of the Reverend Irwine completes the group. He is one of George Eliot's sympathetic portraits of the honorable, effective clergyman, comfortable in his elegant habits but mindful of duties to a widowed mother and sickly sister, and far better for his parishioners than a more dogmatic and consistent man could ever be. The only main character not associated with a particular place in Hayslope is Hetty's cousin, Dinah Morris, a young Methodist minister who lives in Stoniton, a place that, as its name suggests, differs considerably from Hayslope.

These various households, linked by a common social order, differ in their particular habits but all rest complacently on the sense that their communal ways, confirmed over centuries, are the right, indeed the only, ways. They all belong to the same community, go to the same church on Sunday where they occupy the same places; they observe the same rituals of celebration and sorrow, during Sunday worship, or birthdays, or funerals, or midsummer and harvest feasts. It is a concentric universe whose rhythmic harmonies, George Eliot makes us feel, have remained undisturbed for centuries. The problem in Hayslope is not absence of community, but absence of self-consciousness and responsibility about community, and consequently, a fatal lack of control over it. They mistakenly associate their customs with the natural events with which their livelihoods are so closely bound, and thus they do not recognize their cultural independence from nature and necessity.

The opening scene is a perfect example of this attitude. It opens in the carpenter's workshop where Adam works in the sunlight, his plane sending out pine-wood shaving to mingle their scent with the elder-bushes outside the open windows, and his voice intermittently singing a hymn. The whole scene—the carpenter's work, the sunshine, the song of religious celebration—has the serenity characteristic of Adam and his community, the serenity of people untroubled in their larger views. The sunshine itself seems to guarantee the human light of intention and reverence. But even as these circumstances are being introduced, we follow the flirtation between the young lord and the dairymaid that eventually will dissipate the sunshine and alter the basic conditions of life in Hayslope.

The only oblique notes in book 1 apart from this flirtation are introduced with Dinah Morris. It is she who comes to comfort the widowed Lisbeth Bede, to warn and comfort Hetty, and to bring the community her message as a preacher. Her ventures into Hayslope bring glimpses of another, darker world, as if even the beauty of Hayslope nature were partly a reflex of the human richness in its midst. When the people gather on the common to hear Dinah preach, they come together for something new and quite different from their customary ritual celebrations and observances, and they exercise in new ways their private consciences. The second book, however, introduces various oblique perspectives and brings the viewpoints of various outsiders more to bear on the circumstances. These include the narrator, who discourses on the importance of common life, Mr. Irwine as seen from a perspective much later than the events of this story, and Bartle Massey, the night-school teacher, who is an outsider in Hayslope. Bartle lives on the edge of town and at night teaches the illiterate farmers and artisans of Hayslope how to read and write and do sums. In different ways both he and Dinah reflect the extensive power of the Evangelical revival in encouraging the rural population to learn: both how to work with their own heads rather than relying on the thinking of others, and how to gain the tools for self-governance, beginning with reading the Bible but, as in Bartle's school, extending far beyond. These two characters, however, remain marginal to the central events until those events blow apart the community's confidence in its "natural" ways.

Book 3 deals exclusively with the birthday feast for Arthur Donnithorne, a ritual celebration that is a long timeless moment in the novel. The dinner, the health-drinking, the games, and the dance all have their time-honored protocols and celebrate the renewal of a traditional, even feudal social organization. It is completely appropriate in such a vision that the point of view is handed to the older gentry, looking on this confirmation of an entire order. But even here, in the contacts between Arthur and Hetty, are clear hints of another agenda and another order of event. In book 4, time and the processes it unfolds threaten the timeless order with the consequences of secret life, consequences that become public knowledge in book 5 after Hetty has fled her engagement to Adam and fled Hayslope in search of Arthur.

The chief events of the plot are events that often are assumed to be natural—Arthur's seduction of Hetty, the birth of her baby, its death—and yet there is an almost complete suppression of natural explanation. None of the events just mentioned is represented in the novel. They are unmistakably foreshadowed, and their harsh, inexorable consequences are felt, but they remain invisible, as if outside the margins of consciousness in the text. George Eliot elides these events, not because she shrinks from the facts of life—a brief summary of *Adam Bede* disarms that speculation—but because she saw these events as the results of other, more powerful, less visible, events taking place in individual consciousness. The physical results of these private motives are concrete, indisputable, given, but they result from the operation of cultural processes of motivation and intention that are less visible but more complex and just as real. These are the more important focus of attention. As always in her fiction, moral life is a process, not a point. To consider events apart from these conditions is a potent kind of exclusiveness that is as vulgar and that distorts perception of the common ground just as much as doctrines and snobbery do. She deliberately minimizes the melodramatic, the heroic, the discrete event—what she calls the "vulgar coercion of conventional plot"[17]—in order to concentrate on the links between events in those ideas people carry around with them, light as air but powerful as acid or sunlight. The event as incarnation is her constant object of focus. Ideas and acts are not separate; what we think, we do not necessarily do, but we rarely do something without precedents in consciousness and memory. In *Adam Bede* she follows most closely the development of such compelling precedents, especially in Arthur Donnithorne.

In Arthur's case, the precedents are simultaneously cultural and personal. The wicket gate that is "never opened" (ch. 6), the one between the Hall and the farm, is the one Hetty and Arthur use for their secret meetings; it is also a symbol of the illicit connection, the classic privilege of lordship—a custom so barbarous that Arthur would be horrified to be associated with it, and yet it is a convention he revives by his actions as if it has wrought itself into his habitual thought in ways he is unconscious of and does not allow for. Despite his individual self-consciousness and good intentions, his story is an obvious traditional tale of the lord and the dairymaid, and he acts it out as if he had a script. What is at stake is not so much the compulsion of tradition as it is the way tradition itself and even legend arises from and is reconfirmed in the actions of individual men and women.

George Eliot remorselessly exposes the slow but certain process of Arthur's self-betrayal, and consequently betrayal of the community in which order depends upon his exertion of his proper function. His idea of himself as noble patron, on the brink of assuming his role as

feudal master, and full of optimistic visions of himself in various acts
of generosity, conflicts with his temptation to seduce the maid he
knows he never will marry. Liking to believe in only one alternative,
he does not hearken to the real presence of another. "He no sooner
fixed his mind on the probable consequence of giving way to the emotions which had stolen over him . . . than he refused to believe such
a future for himself" (p. 139; ch. 13). Though he vacillates between
two minds, his behavior is increasingly of a piece. Like "many men
since his day" he rides a long way to avoid a meeting with Hetty,
"and then galloped hastily back lest he should miss it" (p. 129; ch.
12). He loses himself wilfully, enjoying the oblivion, as does Hetty,
with her "narcotic daydreams" of being married and a great lady.
Whatever he may intend, what he does is what counts, and George
Eliot brilliantly examines the process whereby thought and action go
separate ways.

This is not what he meant to say. His arm is stealing round the waist again,
it is tightening its clasp; he is bending his face nearer and nearer to the
round cheek, his lips are meeting those pouting child-lips, and for a long
moment time has vanished. He may be a shepherd in Arcadia for aught he
knows, he may be the first youth kissing the first maiden, he may be Eros
himself, sipping the lips of Psyche—it is all one.
      There was no speaking for minutes after. They walked along with beating
hearts till they came within sight of the gate at the end of the wood. Then
they looked at each other, not quite as they had looked before, for in their
eyes there was the memory of a kiss. (p. 138; ch. 13)

In widening the scope to include mythic precedents George Eliot's
narrator not only suggests a certain kind of sensation, but also suggests the way in which it momentarily obliterates the individual
awareness. As personal memory disappears and with it the history
that involves consequences, we momentarily lose the sense of choice
and willed action. Arthur recovers himself after Hetty is gone, but he
cannot resist losing himself again and again. Like Janet Dempster
with her bottle of brandy, and like characters in all the novels who
rely on gambling or moral superiority or daydreams, Arthur takes the
opiate of delusion and absolves him of responsibility for his own actions, leaving them to the mercy of his changeable desires. He cannot
govern his actions because he will not accept the fact that both of his
conflicting desires cannot be satisfied. To be the rightful lord of the

estate requires him to fulfill a trust to his friends. He betrays this trust when he seduces Hetty, good intentions notwithstanding. Good intentions, not acted upon, have no power compared with the intentions evident in his actual behavior, however he may wish it otherwise.

What Arthur does in particular can be determined only by him, but he could be hindered or influenced by others. As it happens, and because things are complex in human situations to begin with, and because each person is satisfied with his own picture of circumstances, Arthur's friends do not guess the problem in time. Adam believes that the flirtation is superficial and that Hetty's blushes are for him, "having woven for himself an ingenious web of probabilities, the surest screen a wise man can place between himself and the truth" (p. 295; ch. 26). Arthur determines to confess to Reverend Irwine but his determination is weakened by a series of deflections and he deflects again for fear of looking like a fool. "The idea of Hetty had just crossed Mr. Irwine's mind as he looked inquiringly at Arthur, but his disclaiming, indifferent answer confirmed the thought . . . that there could be nothing serious in that direction. There was no probability that Arthur ever saw her except at church" (p. 176; ch. 16). Even Dinah, possessed of some instinct to warn Hetty of trouble, only succeeds in annoying and frightening her. And so Arthur and Hetty maintain a life apart, and after Arthur's departure with his regiment, Hetty supports her secret alone. She disappears in search of Arthur, Adam follows in pursuit of false leads, Hetty seeks Dinah in Stoniton after failing to find Arthur, but Dinah has gone elsewhere. As she fades from our view she has become an alienated, scarcely human creature of "objectless wandering, apart from all love, caring for human beings only through her pride, clinging to life only as the hunted wounded brute clings to it" (p. 398; ch. 38). The terror of her solitude, the pathos of her dependence on the community she has contemptuously left behind make Hetty's value and the anguish of her helplessness exquisitely felt.

As customary usage begins to appear less "natural" and more problematic, and as the possibilities outside customary usage appear stronger, the marginal figures of Dinah and Bartle assume increasing importance. Unlike the other characters, each has a vocation that does not depend on the structure of custom in Hayslope, and so after custom has fallen away they still have a clear sense of purpose and have the freedom that attends it. As the pressures on customary ways intensify they become mediators, helping Adam and Hetty to imagine and accept alternatives. They are instruments of resignation that enable Adam and Hetty to gain control of their actions once again by beginning with their acceptance of the actual events in which they have been willing or unwilling participants.

Adam's case is not the most moving, but it is especially interesting because his strong sense of vocation and duty has none of the sympathy or fellow-feeling that might be expected to attend such commitment. He has little of the flexibility of the more artistic man of purpose painting his picture with an idea independent of specific results. His strengths have a "correlative hardness" (p. 214; ch. 19) that makes him humorless and short of patience. He shrinks from the suffering, imprisoned Hetty as if he were a cruel man, and his first response to the news of her arrest for child murder is, "'It *can't be!*'" (p. 417; ch. 39). But it not only can be, it is; what "ought" to be crumbles in the face of it. Bartle's ministrations are ungentle but effective in getting Adam past his inability to accept the fact. And his acceptance gives him a new consciousness beside which his old seems narrow and weak. The narrator describes the final result of this process in Adam in terms that evoke George Eliot's description of the artist in life, the one who follows an idea like the Evangelical conception of duty. "The growth of higher feeling within us is like the growth of faculty, bringing with it a sense of added strength: we can no more wish to return to a narrower sympathy, than a painter or a musician can wish to return to his cruder manner, or a philosopher to his less complete formula" (p. 541; ch. 54). "I used to be hard sometimes," Adam tells Bartle at Hetty's trial, but "I'll never be hard again" (p. 439; ch. 42).

Hetty's case is the most dramatic and painful because she is least prepared to cope with the violent changes she endures—abandonment in her pregnancy, the physical trauma of childbirth, the death of her baby, the prolonged psychological trauma of someone coping for the first time with anonymity and solitude, the humiliation of a public trial and of imprisonment, and the threat of execution. Here again the heaviest burden falls on the one least able to bear it. Mrs. Poyser complains early in the novel that "her heart's as hard as a pebble" (p. 158; ch. 15), but like Caterina, Hetty's anomalous position isolates her in a family where blood ties are everything; and her demonstrable incapacity for sympathy is not entirely surprising in a community based on hierarchical social bonds rather than on a sense of common ground. When she reappears at her trial, after disappearing from our view, she has the same remoteness and habits of concealment that undid her initially. Her "hard" heart gives up its secrets only on the eve of her execution after Dinah has come to her cell. There Hetty at first seems "like an animal that gazes, and gazes, and keeps aloof," but she clings to the "human contact" of Dinah's hand, a contact that finally invades her reserve. The brightness of the opening chapters has disappeared completely, along with the leisurely rhythms of the opening books. The pace has accumulated speed, contracting to a point "in that grey clear morning, when the fatal cart with the two young women in it was descried by the waiting watching multitude, cleaving its way towards the hideous symbol of a deliberately-inflicted sudden death" (p. 472; ch. 47). At this vertiginous moment, the last-minute reprieve that saves Hetty from the gallows for a more lingering death as a transported criminal, is brought through the crowd at a gallop by Arthur Donnithorne. By this point the entire style of the novel has unsettled the easy assumption made by the citizens of Hayslope that their ways belong somehow to the eternal nature of things.

While Adam and Hetty have painfully endured the loss of their dreams and the acceptance of harsh facts, Arthur has used his privilege in an attempt to prevent himself from losing any alternatives; his will and his way are one, or so he thinks. The degree of his self-absorption is stressed by the brilliant stroke of having Arthur shifted from one world to another abruptly. He leaves Hayslope complacently looking forward to returning as its master. As he steps off the coach after months of absence he positively savors his own "good nature." "Arthur had not an evil feeling in his mind towards any human being: he was happy, and would make every one else happy that came within his reach." Considering that Hetty is in jail awaiting execution, his friends are in disgrace and despair as a consequence of his actions, nothing could be more odious than this narcissistic fantasy, and nothing more false than his good intentions. His first thought is to refresh himself, his second to sit on his velvet cushion to open his letters, the first being a letter from Mr. Irwine marked urgent. "With an agreeable anticipation of soon seeing the writer, Arthur breaks the seal and reality breaks in on him.

"I send this letter to meet you. . . . I will not attempt to add by one word
of reproach to the retribution that is now falling on you: any other words
that I could write at this moment must be weak and unmeaning by the side
of those in which I must tell you the simple fact.

"Hetty Sorrel is in prison, and will be tried on Friday for the crime of
child murder. . . ." (pp. 451-54; ch. 45)

The recognition of what his actions mean, the recognition that he *is*
what he has done regardless of intentions, the recognition that he has
deliberately trod the path away from his own dreams, all dawn on
Arthur too late to change more than Hetty's sentence. The "simple
fact" is the incarnation of his will and his intention and no wishing
can remove this unaccommodating actual fact. The private, invisible
habits that permit him to overstep his own acknowledged bounds do
not remain invisible forever. With the changes that he helps to bring
into being, a whole public way of life is permanently altered.

Book 6 is more muted and restrained than the opening book. The
glad, bright morning belonged to a confidence founded on unreliable
illusions and visions of action out of touch with the facts of ambition,
secret indulgence, and complacency about the commonplace things
that bind together separate lives. The novel demonstrates the truth of
Mr. Irwine's observations to Adam and to Arthur that people cannot
isolate themselves. "Men's lives are as thoroughly blended with each
other as the air they breathe" (p. 434; ch. 51), and our actions have
consequences that are "hardly ever confined to ourselves" (p. 175; ch.
16). Human influence extends to all perception, even perception of
nature. One of the striking accomplishments of this novel is the way
George Eliot links the vision of natural beauty with the social harmony in its midst. Hetty's example is the most extended. She blos-
soms in a security she takes for granted in Hayslope. In the supremely
domestic context of the dairy farm, her beauty is the delicate, fragile
beauty of "kittens, or very small downy ducks making gentle rippling
noises with their soft bills, or babies just beginning to toddle."
When she leaves the world of dairy sounds and sunshine she enters a
cold, ugly, dark world where her beauty disappears, as if she passes
from the world of light and speech to what might as well be a grave.
In the darkness outside her society her beauty disappears immediately, as if at the snap of some magician's fingers an enchanted world
had vanished. In "the horror of this cold, and darkness, and solitude—out of all human reach," where she can barely make out the

rapid motion of some creature in the field, where she lies in a "hovel of furze" Hetty's beauty vanishes with her vitality. "It was almost as if she were dead already, and knew that she was dead, and longed to get back to life again" (p. 394; ch. 37). With Hetty's beauty as with Adam's sunny confidence, the tide of events completely changes the appearance of light, as if it and Hetty's beauty and Adam's confidence all are functions of their place in a changeable, even fragile human society.

The Mill on the Floss

The Mill on the Floss (1860) gives fuller presentation than her first novel to that "conflict of valid claims" that is one hallmark of George Eliot's fiction. This new fullness may be what she referred to when she wrote to her friend, and French translator Francois D'Albert Durade, "there is more thought and a profounder veracity in 'The Mill' than in 'Adam' " (*Letters,* 3:374). This second novel insists on the presence of alternatives in personal and in cultural experience. The central community of St. Oggs on the river Floss contains contradictory ways of life: the one rural, the other fast becoming urban; the one peasant, the other middle-class; the one feudal, the other mercantile. She anticipates here (even more clearly than in *Adam Bede*) her strategy in all future novels, that of showing a new order appearing on the margins of an old. Just as Evangelicalism alters Milby (so do election reform in *Felix Holt* and the railroads in *Middlemarch*) so the wharves and machinery of St. Oggs mark an impending social change in the rural community of farmers and millers central to the story of Maggie Tulliver and her brother Tom.

Within the Dodson and Tulliver family, however, the sense of alternatives is remarkably attenuated, and this narrowness insidiously forecloses on the freedom of children like Maggie and Tom to develop their fullest human powers, or even to develop the power of survival. The Dodson-Tulliver clan recalls George Eliot's discussion of the "clan" in her essay on the Germany peasantry, and recalls her comment on cultural development in her review of Mackay's *The Progress of the Intellect.* Their civilization is a blending of living ideas with "lifeless barbarisms" descended to them "like so many petrifactions from distant ages." They "are in bondage to terms and conceptions which, having had their root in conditions of thought no longer existing, have ceased to possess any vitality, and are for [a new age] as spells which have lost their virtue" (*Essays,* 28). These Dodsons and Tullivers are "very simple people, who had never had any illuminating doubts as to personal integrity and honour."[18] They elevate family tradition to a universal principal of "right" and exclude all other possibilities or alternatives as simply "wrong." A Dodson omits nothing "that belonged to the eternal fitness of things which was plainly indicated in the practice of the most substantial parishioners, and in the family traditions—such as, obedience to parents, faithfulness to kindred, industry, rigid honesty, thrift, the thorough scouring of wooden and copper utensils, the hoarding of coins likely to disappear from the currency, the production of first-rate commodities for the market, and the general preference for whatever was home-made" (*Floss,* pp. 240–41; book 4, ch. 1). There is only one point of view on all matters, the "right" one, and that one is "whatever is customary and respectable"; all others lie in a dim twilight zone outside their well-lit parlors. Two points of view, if they are "right," are merely replications of a single point of view. Mrs. Glegg, for example, "had both a front and a back parlour in her excellent house at St. Oggs, so that she had two points of view from which she could observe the weaknesses of her fellow-beings, and reinforce her thankfulness for her own exceptional strength of mind" (*Floss,* p. 107; book 1, ch. 12). The Dodson sisters are so particular about their customs, and so chary of all change, that they continue to refer to themselves as "Dodsons" long after they have been married—one to Deane the banker, two to Pullet and Glegg, men with good business heads and customary views, and one, Maggie and Tom's mother, to Tulliver the miller. George Eliot's portraits of these different households, and of the family gatherings, are full of wit and amusement. It is increasingly clear, however, that though they avoid the worst failures of free-lance egoism, and though they admit of a common ground among themselves that allows for strict rules, their very integrity is based on an exclusiveness that has more strength than vitality in a new generation. For them truth is absolute, not provisional, and entirely consistent with their own views. No opposing claims could have validity.

The aim or purpose of such people, what Feuerbach would call their religion, not only operates by exclusion, but also depends on material existence; it is bound to place and to particular things and does not survive their loss. The connections between details and what amounts to religious dogma is one of the amusements of the detailed family portraits of the first two books. Aunt Pullet reveals her new bonnet to her sister and nieces with the kind of reverential, ritual attention accorded only to religious relics (book 1, ch. 9); and the items of Mrs. Tulliver's household dowry—her silver and linen, china and skewers, all carefully kept in her private closet—are to her what the teraphim were to the ancient Hebrews: "household gods" or idols representing the spirits of the place (book 3, ch. 2). The mill and its lands have the same value for Mr. Tulliver. These objects are the places, or sites, or repositories of all meaning and value, the abstract and the particular being mixed in much the same way as they are in the family values, which include both obedience to parents and the thorough scouring of copper utensils. When absolute value is associated in this way with particular objects, there is little basis for recognizing a common ground with others unlike oneself. The "emmet-like" Dodsons and Tullivers have that "spirit of communal exclusiveness—the resistance to the indiscriminate establishment of strangers," that identifies the intensely traditional peasant in the essay on "The Natural History of German Life."[19] The Dodson and Tulliver world is divided into categories of "kin" and "no kin," and any flexibility on this score they regard as moral weakness. The habits of mind are amusing in Aunt Pullet's bonnet worship, but more ominous in Mr. Tulliver's obsession for revenge against "lawyer Wakem" after losing his mill and land, especially when the oath of revenge and the ambition to recover the property is inscribed in the family Bible and made a central guide for his son's life. Tulliver feels no need to accept inconvenience, no need for resignation, and so his actions become increasingly quixotic and self-destructive.

While the Dodson's and Tullivers feud, the narrator quietly extends the readers' awareness beyond these narrow margins with evidence belonging to other places and times, extending the perception of common ground between the town of St. Oggs and German river villages, between the lives of factory workers and those of "good society," between the sunshine of childhood and the wilderness of adult cares, between Homer's heroes and the Tulliver children. The Duke of Wellington, Novalis, Prince Hamlet of Denmark, and other such subjects appear in the margins of the story in comments such as the following one, widening the sense of connectedness:

I share with you the sense of this oppressive narrowness; but it is necessary that we should feel it if we care to understand how it acted on the lives of Tom and Maggie—how it has acted on young natures in many

generations . . . for does not science tell us that its highest striving is after
the ascertainment of a unity which shall bind the smallest things with the
greatest? In natural science, I have understood, there is nothing petty to the
mind that has a large vision of relations, and to which every single object
suggests a vast sum of conditions. It is surely the same with the observation
of human life. (*Floss,* pp. 238–39; book 4, ch. 1)

Calling attention to the wider life, and to its own activity, this mind
presents itself as a model: consulting facts, self-aware, painting a picture, inclusive rather than exclusive, considering how things are
rather than how they ought to be. This voice counteracts the clan narrowness with a sense of the wider possibilities lying outside St. Oggs
and just beyond Maggie Tulliver's reach.

The main story concerns the events and conditions shaping Maggie's possibilities as she grows from childhood and comes of age.
George Eliot's only novel focusing on childhood, *The Mill on the Floss*
demonstrates in the most elemental way how the habits of an entire
society become part of the internalized equipment of children before
they reach the point of conscious choice. The first two books present
"Boy and Girl," and their "School Time." Tulliver opens the second
chapter with a discussion about educating his children and it is already clear in this chapter which way things are tending. Tom, whose
talents and interest lie in farming, will go to school because he is a
boy: his future occupation will provide considerable help to his father
in dealing with "raskill" lawyers. Maggie, whose talents and interests
lie with books and pictures, will stay home because she is a girl. Thus
for Maggie there is a continual conflict between what her family tells
her she "ought" to be, and what her instincts tell her she *is*. Maggie's
constant frustration is that nothing about her fits the category she
supposedly was born for. Unlike her cousin Lucy, perfect in dress and
demeanor, with hair that stays curled, with a truly sweet, docile disposition, Maggie gets mud on her pinafore and jostles into things,
her straight hair refuses to curl and her enthusiasms are continually
running her afoul of the "eternal fitness of things." She is not a "proper" girl, "like other folks's children." Maggie learns from an early
age that she is always "wrong," and her powers of defiance are feeble
against the collected forces of her family. Her mother is not her ally;
Elizabeth Tulliver is a model of amiability and dull-wittedness, and
was chosen by her overbearing husband for precisely those qualities.

Not being "right" Maggie dares to be wrong, occasionally, in her childhood, but she has no allies. Her decided actions, calculated to make virtues of necessity—such as ducking the uncooperative curls in water, or cutting them off altogether—meet with a "chorus of reproach and derision." Her mother, her brother, her aunts and uncles continually remind her that she must be "right" if she wishes to be loved.

Unlike Antigone, Maggie does not know how to urge the validity of her claims in opposition to the forces ranged against her. Maggie's desire to do the "right" thing is early associated with a neurotic "need to be loved, the strongest need in poor Maggie's nature" (*Floss*, p. 34; book 1; ch. 5), and this need triumphs over her pride again and again. She substitutes another's will, even her brother's, for her own and learns to distrust her personal inclination whenever it is in conflict with others. When she forgets to feed Tom's rabbits, and he renounces her—"I don't love you"—Maggie begs, " O Tom, please forgive me—I can't bear it—I will always be good—always remember things—do love me—please dear Tom!" Her need for love overthrows her pride and with it her integrity. She cannot exercise independent judgment. She will promise to be something she cannot be (always good, always remember things): anything, so long as the essential support is not withdrawn. Her need for love is a morbid dependency, and Tom uses it to master her, threatening to hate her if she is not just what he requires.[20]

Her brother, Tom, unhampered by being "wrong" in this way, puts himself continually in the other available category. At the age of thirteen he is already "clear and positive on one point—namely, that he would punish everybody who deserved it: why, he wouldn't have minded being punished himself, if he deserved it; but, then, he never *did* deserve it" (*Floss*, p. 35; book 1, ch. 5). He is very fond of his sister; "he meant always to take care of her, make her his housekeeper, and punish her when she did wrong." His conception of the whole duty of woman is cruder than his father's or his teacher's, but essentially the same. Reverend Stelling, to whom Tom goes to school, teaches his subject in "the right way, indeed he knew no other," and his opinions consist perfectly with this mental habit, including the opinion that girls are "quick and shallow" and "couldn't go far in anything" (*Floss*, p. 134; book 2, ch. 1). Wakem, the objectionable lawyer, holds a view of women perfectly consistent with that of the

Tulliver clan; "we don't ask what a woman does," he says, "we ask whom she belongs to" (*Floss*, p. 372; book 6, ch. 8), with a coarseness he seems entirely unaware of.

The only time Tom begins to develop a sense of alternatives, and hence of the questionable value of his customary ways and familial "rights," is at Stelling's school, where the different "standard of things" domestic and personal acts like a difference of native language, casting his whole moral vocabulary in question. "For the first time in his life he had a painful sense that he was all wrong somehow" and this "nullified his boyish self-satisfaction and gave him something like a girl's susceptibility" (*Floss*, p. 121; book 2, ch. 1). His new perspective on himself is enlarged by the presence of Philip Wakem, son of the lawyer (Mr. Tulliver chose this very school in a competitive spirit). Although Philip has a hunch back, he can do everything with ease that Tom cannot do at all, especially draw pictures, and Tom's usual physical mode of establishing superiority by fighting has no place in his school existence. He is even forced to admire Philip. But nothing in Tom's previous education has countered the "narrow tendency in his mind to details" (p. 145; book 2, ch. 3), and nothing has encouraged either him or his sister to move from particulars to the larger relations among things that would help to explain those particulars. Their reaction to Tom's Latin grammar suggests this limitation forcibly. In his despair about learning Latin, Tom even tries prayer as a resort, and eventually he concludes Latin is "beastly" stuff. Maggie skips the "rules of the Syntax—the examples became so absorbing" (p. 131; book 2, ch. 1). Neither Tom nor Maggie learns enough about the syntax of things, or about the differences between one syntax and another, to overcome their earliest lessons about exclusiveness, obedience, and passivity.

The next three books shift the balance away from the scenes of childhood showing how Maggie and Tom run afoul of the family rigidities, and toward a world of change where the family rigidities run afoul of some hard, unaccommodating facts. The tone of this new departure is suggested by the book titles: book 3, "The Downfall," book 4, "The Valley of Humiliation," and book 5, "Wheat and Tares." An age-old story is being drawn here, beginning with the loss of paradise and innocence. "They had entered the thorny wilderness, and the golden gates of their childhood had for ever closed behind them" (p. 171; book 2, ch. 7). Mr. Tulliver's obsession with his "rights" at home and abroad has involved him in litigations, and when he finally loses a litigation over some dykes, he is forced to pay for his losses by negotiating a loan from his Dodson kin; when this negotiation turns into a feud—a faint echo of feudal wars of hereditary "right"— his unsatisfied creditors sell his property. By attempting to force his tradition on others by forcing law on the side of tradition, Mr. Tulliver destroys the traditional place that secured him. The story concerns the family's response to this unthinkable, unanticipated, wholly "impossible" change.

Both children endure very young the loss of their familiar world, without its familiar objects, in a house no longer theirs, and with parents stricken by misfortune into dullness and even illness. Mrs. Tulliver compounds the disaster by attempting to turn the tide. Her natural ignorance having been cultivated by her husband, it bears fruit at the moment when illness relaxes his control over her, and brings on the coup de grace, the sale of the mill to Wakem. Wakem, who had no thought of such an action until Mrs. Tulliver puts it into his head by begging him to avoid it, is "not without his parenthetic vindictiveness towards the uncomplimentary miller" that enables him to take advantage of his old enemy without going to trouble. Tom's opportunity at school having come to a premature close, the boy concentrates his interest "into the one channel of ambitious resistance to misfortune" (p. 242; book 4, ch. 3), guided by his father's wish for revenge. Having lived as they liked, and having been deprived of that possibility in the most humiliating way, all Tom and his father can think of is to restore the past circumstances. Action based on resignation is unthinkable.

Maggie, on the other hand, wants some principle of explanation, and thinks she finds it in a book, brought by an old playfellow, Bob Jakin. Using Thomas a Kempis's *The Imitation of Christ* as her "master key" to life, Maggie resolves to meet misfortune by "plans of self-humiliation and entire devotedness." She succeeds so well that her mother is amazed "that this once 'contrary' child was become so submissive, so backward to assert her own will" (pp. 255–57; book 4, ch. 3). But the motives are still what they were, despite the high-mindedness. There is the familiar connection between devotion and self-humiliation. As the narrator has warned, her rebelliousness is weaker than her need to be loved and it has turned into a strange passivity. She still turns against herself in order to be right, but now she can do it on principle. This is the opposite of resignation because it is an end in itself, not a prologue to a particular course of action.

The morbidity of this so-called renunciation is obvious to Philip Wakem, who has befriended her in secret, and with whom she shares her interest in music and books behind the backs of their families. "It is mere cowardice," he tells Maggie, "to seek safety in negations. No character becomes strong in that way." With a certain self-interest at stake he argues that "it is less wrong that you should see me than that you should be committing this long suicide," but his self-interest, while it complicates Maggie's difficulties, does not invalidate the accuracy of his observation (pp. 287–88; book 5, ch. 3). The stolen good that Maggie receives from this friendship is a balm to her sensibility, and yet suspect and problematic as well, not only because Philip's feelings are more intense than hers, but also because it mixes up wrong and right confusingly. What is "right" for her is "wrong" to her family and must be carried on in secret, if at all. Her relief at discovery, and the end of her meetings with Philip, is largely the relief that conflict and choice are over. But even this resolution is problematic. "If she had felt that she was entirely wrong, and that Tom had been entirely right, she could sooner have recovered more inward harmony" (p. 305; book 5, ch. 6). She has not learned to control conflict, and to choose between alternatives. "I flutter in all ways, and fly in none" (p. 286; book 5, ch. 3), she complains to Philip. She defends herself against Tom with reference to the impossibility of her having a vocation; he can do something in particular because, she says, "you are a man . . . and have power, and can do something in the world." He replies coldly, "Then if you can do nothing, submit to those that can" (p. 304; book 5, ch. 5). This book, "Wheat and Tares," concerns the mixed effect of every sowing: of Maggie's beneficial and yet disastrous friendship with Philip; of Tom's long, deliberate effort to redeem the family property. The surprise announcement that he has done so with secret investments made with the help of Bob Jakin and his aunt, produces both the long-awaited "reckoning" with creditors and also the unexpected reckoning between Mr. Tulliver and his mortality. The shock of success kills the father, just when things seem to promise most fairly. In such a world, Maggie's habit of "fluttering in all ways" is more realistic than Tom's inexorable plodding in a fixed track.

Maggie's instinct for something better than narrow motives and narrow clan definitions moves her beyond her brother's grim almost mechanical pursuits, but it does not move her far enough. She must ground her instinct outside this world, doing something in particular, if she is to escape from its grasp on her mind and feelings. A vague instinct for "fuller music" will not secure her, without some idea of her own, which gives her aim and purpose. The narrator speaks directly of this need in a passage that, characteristically, widens the scope of Maggie's struggle and locates its place in a wider scheme of things:

In writing the history of unfashionable families, one is apt to fall into a tone of emphasis which is very far from being the tone of good society, where principles and beliefs are not only of an extremely moderate kind, but are always presupposed, no subjects being eligible but such as can be touched with a light and graceful irony. But then, good society has its claret and its velvet carpets, its dinner engagements six weeks deep, its opera and its faery ballrooms; rides off its ennui on thoroughbred horses, lounges at the club, has to keep clear of crinoline vortices, gets its science done by Faraday, and its religion by the superior clergy who are to be met in the best houses: how should it have time or need for belief and emphasis? But good society, floated on gossamer wings of light irony, is of very expensive production; requiring nothing less than a wide and arduous national life condensed in unfragrant deafening factories, cramping itself in mines, sweating at furnaces, grinding, hammering, weaving under more or less oppression or carbonic acid—or else, spread over sheepwalks, and scattered in lonely houses and huts on the clayey or chalky corn-lands, where the rainy days look dreary. This wide national life is based entirely on emphasis—the emphasis of want, which urges it into all the activities necessary for the maintenance of good society and light irony: it spends it heavy years often in a chill, uncarpeted fashion, amidst family discord unsoftened by long corridors. (pp. 255–56; book 4, ch. 3)

Good society, that is, bases its plenitude palpably on the want of others, a fact as invisible to the aristocratic peasant as it is to the humbler variety. This passage states explicitly the connectedness of human culture and the inevitable conflict of valid claims. Even unspeculative minds require relief from want, some "outside standing-ground" if not in art, then in enthusiasm, or emphatic belief, or gin. This extensive common life—evident here and elsewhere through the narrator's presence—sharpens the sense of Maggie's difficulty, as she reaches out from a narrow solitude for a reality that is everywhere apparent in the text but that, in her circumstances, has no accepted name or definition: a reality to which ultimately there is no access for her because her circumstances are too powerful and her struggle too solitary.

Two characters in *The Mill on the Floss,* Philip Wakem and Bob Jakin, manage to circumvent the narrowness of life in St. Oggs, and, artistlike, to determine their course by using circumstances as they find them. Both are male and both are outsiders in that they are marginal to St. Oggs society, and they are potentially citizens of that larger world evident in the narrator's diversifying allusions to biblical precendent, scientific conceptions, classical literature, or political history. Philip Wakem, who is by vocation an artist, has learned from physical debility how to work with frustration, and the patience that first appears in his artist's discipline appears in his personal affairs most clearly when he announces to his father that he wishes to marry Maggie Tulliver, daughter of the enemy. Wakem's rage does not deflect Philip or unsettle him—"I expected all this"—and he chooses his time so as gradually to bring his father around from outright refusal to actual agreement (p. 372; book 6, ch. 8), a small miracle in which he has the estimable assistance of Lucy Deane, Maggie's cousin. Bob Jakin, the childhood friend and traveling salesman who brings Maggie presents of books, proves his power by overcoming Aunt Glegg's resistance to purchasing from his wares. He accomplishes this radical innovation, in the time-honored method of radicals, by pitching to her weak spot, and using her perspective against her: something he can only do because he knows what her perspective is, exactly what it is and exactly how unflattering to himself. He, too, "expected this" when she resists (p. 280; book 5, ch. 2), and so he, too, is ready to act. Though the episode is one of comic relief, its point is not trivial. Bob and Philip share a sense of alternatives and a patience in pursuing a chosen object that distinguish them from Tom, who sees no alternatives, and from Maggie, who has no steady purpose (who sees too many). Maggie recognizes the existence of conflict, but she merely internalizes it without developing a purpose of her own.

The last two books demonstrate inexorably what must be the outcome of such a history as Maggie and Tom's. "The Great Temptation" (book 6) finds Maggie a young woman, and returned on vacation from her "dreary situation in a school" (p. 318; book 6, ch. 1). Being a governess, which many in the nineteenth century rightly regarded as the last refuge of despair, is nevertheless a job Maggie has taken in order to be independent. This commendable aim, and the circumstance of her first employment, remain unrepresented; they are entirely outside the plot. Her temptation comes in the shape of

Stephen Guest, Lucy Deane's undeclared fiancé and the richest, best looking young bachelor in St. Oggs. The suggestion to Maggie that here she may find relief from her meager, restricted existence has a powerful influence. "There is something strangely winning to most women in that offer of the firm arm: the help is not wanted physically at that moment, but the sense of help—the presence of strength that is outside them and yet theirs—meets a continual want of the imagination" (p. 356; book 6, ch. 6). Being used to treatment that is indifferent and preemptive, Maggie is all the more susceptible to this promise of a fuller existence; and yet she is uncertain "whether this existence which tempted her *was* the full existence she had dreamed of" (p. 420; book 6, ch. 14). Stephen's self-indulgent character shows this caution to be wise, and yet the promises he represents are quite real. When they have drifted into flirtation, and then farther, circumstances throw them together in such a way as to be compromising to Maggie's reputation. Though they are innocent, Stephen has allowed them to get into such difficulties in the hope of forcing Maggie to marry him; he argues, falsely enough, that it is "natural" to act on their mutual attraction—"It has come upon us without our seeking: it is natural" and that "the natural law surmounts all others" (p. 393; book 6, ch. 11). Maggie has rejected Philip on just such grounds, that her family has "natural claims" on her. The falseness of both arguments appears most clearly by the time Maggie confronts Stephen, because what binds her to her ties in St. Oggs is clearly unnatural in the extreme (i.e., cultural), and a product of decades, even centuries of cultivation.

But though the natural claim is invalid, Stephen's claim is not necessarily invalid. When Maggie departs for St. Oggs, she does not reason about it; it is that her "heart" won't let her. The past is her "stay" and yet, when she returns to her home she is outcast by everyone. She returns to a town that refuses to accept her, but she cannot imagine a life outside it. The "right" way is clearly impossible to find, and yet Maggie keeps looking for it. The last chapters find her waiting for "the light that would surely come" (p. 450; book 7, ch. 5). The idea of rescue keeps her in place, and as she prays to God for guidance, alternately accepting Stephen's letters of proposal and recoiling against her impulse to do so, the fatal flood rises about her knees. "The Final Rescue" (book 7) is another rescue from choice; and this time the final effort at reunion with her brother brings at the same moment reunion and death. She can neither accept her circum-

stances nor act outside them. The idea of rescue only leads her into
the fatal embrace in which she and her brother drown.

George Eliot demonstrates the strengths of Maggie's clan as well as
its weaknesses. She does not encourage readers to fall into the mistake
she finds in her characters, a tendency to self-flattering condemnation
of others that is really a form of detachment. Ultimately the main
issues are at root personal, before they become global, and there is no
convenient evil to identify and scourge, apart from the banality that
lazily, half-unwittingly produces pain and destroys lives.

Plotting covetousness, and deliberate contrivance, in order to compass a selfish end, are nowhere abundant but in the world of the dramatist: they demand too intense a mental action for many of our fellow-parishioners to be
guilty of them. It is easy enough to spoil the lives of our neighbours without
taking so much trouble: we can do it by lazy acquiescence and lazy omission,
by trivial falsities for which we hardly know a reason, by small frauds neu-
tralised by small extravagancies, by maladroit flatteries and clumsily impro-
vised insinuations. (p. 23; book 1, ch. 3)

Contrasting with this laziness is George Eliot's artist, pursuing a particular purpose with disciplined action; and contrasting with the
spoiling result of laziness is the creative result, in which the origina-
tor, by the very particularity of his or her action, establishes a sure
connection with fellow-beings. What she says of the artist can be said
of any persons with an aim, or vocation: they have "a mode of ampli-
fying experience and extending [their] contact with [their] fellow-
men beyond the bounds of [their] personal lot" (*Essays*, 271). The exact, particular achievement, the actual incarnation of intention,
makes a difference, in the most literal sense; and that is the only basis
for connection. As she says somewhat abstractly of artistic form, "fundamentally, form is unlikeness," so that "every difference is
form. . . . But with this fundamental discrimination is born in necessary antithesis the sense of wholeness or unbroken connexion in
space & time."[21] The discovery of a difference is the discovery of the
grounds for a connection, and knowledge of difference is essential to
the sympathy between fellow-beings that sustains their common human enterprise. The narrator continually carries the reader's mind
back and forth across such boundaries, reinforcing the sense of connection that such perception brings.

The narrating sensibility, unlike the Dodsons and Tullivers of the
novel, has some of the powers of what she calls elsewhere the "culti-

vated" person. She describes such a person in her essay on "Silly Novels by Lady Novelists," where she contrasts the insipid conventional heroine with the cultivated woman.

> A really cultured woman, like a really cultured man, is all the simpler and the less obtrusive for her knowledge; it has made her see herself and her opinions in something like just proportions; she does not make it a pedestal from which she flatters herself that she commands a complete view of men and things, but makes it a point of observation from which to form a right estimate of herself. . . . She does not give you information, which is the raw material of culture,—she gives you sympathy, which is its subtlest essence. (*Essays,* 317)

By maintaining her individuality such a person strengthens social cohesion. Her self-understanding, the opposite of egoism, is the strength of ego that commands a view beyond its own limits. Such a woman, a possibility sensed by Maggie Tulliver, secures the life that Maggie seeks in vain, by managing to make a syntax of her own from the conflicts of her circumstances. This accomplishment depends on the sense of just proportions that Maggie Tulliver finds she cannot maintain alone.

Chapter Four
Sympathy: *Romola,*
Silas Marner, Felix Holt

For George Eliot sympathy lies near the heart of moral life. Her particular view of sympathy, one that sometimes has eluded her modern critics, has little to do with selfless benevolence. "We should distrust a man," she wrote, "who sets up shop purely for the good of the community."[1] Such "disinterested officiousness" stands opposed to true acts of sympathy, which involve a difficult psychic negotiation between self and other. Though sympathy is a crucial concern to George Eliot throughout her career it has a special meaning in her middle novels because here her concern about sympathy begins to transform her entire treatment of social and moral problems. In her work sympathy depends absolutely upon a division in the psyche, a split in consciousness that permits two conflicting views to exist simultaneously. This mental division is the material of conscience. Her early novels treat sympathy mainly in terms of the relations between well-acquainted individuals, usually members of the same family or small community. The two middle novels, together with a short tale written during the same period, effect an important shift to the late novels and to their concern with sympathy between people more casually related. Although *Silas Marner* was published before *Romola,* I consider *Romola* first. George Eliot had begun work on her Italian novel before she wrote the shorter tale, and the latter (*Silas Marner*) anticipates the structural orginality of the last novels.

Before turning to *Romola,* a glance at Feuerbach's *Essence of Christianity* will help to suggest the psychic conditions for sympathy. This work (see above, chapter 2) influenced George Eliot directly and, through her translation of it, influenced many of her contemporaries as well. Both she and Feuerbach stress the therapeutic and liberating value of this double consciousness; both suggest its moral and even "sacred" function. In the relevant passage of the *Essence* Feuerbach's immediate subject is prayer. As always in the Feuerbachian equation, mankind replaces God. This transposition between God and the human species is wholly congenial to George Eliot, who believed, as she explained it a friend, that "the idea of God, so far as it has been a high spiritual influence, is the ideal of goodness entirely human (i.e., an exaltation of the human)."[2] This is what Feuerbach has to say about prayer:

> In prayer man addresses God with the word of intimate affection—*Thou*; he thus declares articulately that God is his *alter ego*. . . . He confesses to God, as the being nearest to him, his inmost secret thoughts, his deepest wishes, which otherwise he shrinks from uttering. . . . Prayer is the self-division of man into two beings,—a dialogue of man with himself, with his heart. . . . He makes his heart objective. . . . The other is my *thou*—the relation being reciprocal,—my *alter ego*, man objective to me, the revelation of my own nature, the eye seeing itself.[3]

This self-division signals at once a recognition of personal limitation and an effort to reach beyond that limit. The attitude of prayer, then, is one in which the mind, by recognizing its limitations, passes beyond them toward infinite possibilities of the species. It passes, furthermore, not to a single supernatural Father but to a different kind of divine other—the multiple being of humanity as a whole, that is, of the human species. In it the individual finds the divine echo.

This view of other human beings radically changes an individual's relation to others from what it was in a Christian framework. When fellow creatures replace divinity, they cease to be enemies and become, in the sheer fact of their difference, an infinitely valuable resource. Feuerbach cherishes the "qualitative, critical difference between men" and he faults Christianity because it "extinguishes this qualitative distinction; it sets the stamp on all men alike." Such carelessness about individual differences creates an "exaggerated subjectivity" that cripples moral life.

> If . . . no qualitatively different men exist, or, which is the same thing, if there is no distinction between me and others, if we are all perfectly alike, if my sins are not neutralised by the opposite qualities of other men: then assuredly my sin is a blot of shame which cries up to heaven; a revolting horror which can be exterminated only by extraordinary, superhuman, miraculous means. Happily however, there *is* a natural reconciliation. My fellow man is per se the mediator between me and the sacred idea of the species. . . . My sin is made to shrink within its limits, is thrust back in its nothingness, by the fact that it is only mine, and not that of my fellows.[4]

In other words, the differences between me and my fellow creatures establish both the limits of my own failings and also the marvelous possibilities available to me as a human being. They confirm my possibilities and limit my failures. In this reciprocal relation one individual extends and completes the best possibilities of the other.

This model of individual relationship closely resembles George Eliot's idea of sympathy. In her novels any constructive action must be preceded by the recognition of difference: between oneself and another, or between the differing impulses of one's own complex motivation. The capacity to vacillate in itself does no harm and in fact establishes the possibility for creative action. The fact that Arthur Donnithorne vacillates, for example, does not destroy him; his nemesis is rather a weakness of will in heeding the voice that counsels restraint. It could be said fairly that he does not vacillate enough. Adam Bede's character improves, developing a new sympathy, when he begins to experience inner struggles with himself. Single-minded characters in George Eliot usually resemble, not the virtuous Adam, but Tom Tulliver, or Tito Melema in *Romola,* or Jermyn in *Felix Holt:* characters who are strong by negation and whose very single-mindedness becomes a nemesis. Private imperatives always exist in context for George Eliot and must come to terms with actual cases however much they may differ from the projected ideal. To act in well-meaning ignorance, as Harold Transome does in *Felix Holt,* means to act in a dream that the hard unaccommodating actual will bring crashing down.

In George Eliot, as in Feuerbach, sympathy is the first step of a double imperative: first, to accept unruly circumstances, especially those embodied in neighbors and friends; and second, to act on the basis of this acceptance for some particular end. George Eliot was fond of quoting Comte to the effect that our true destiny is composed of *resignation* and *activity;* of acceptance and knowledge of what cannot be changed regardless of our wishes, and the occupation that consists in building on this foundation.[5] Any vision that disregards the hard unaccommodating actual is an unsympathetic vision and one that usually turns destructive. Only vision respecting that actuality can create order and form. George Eliot's idea of sympathy, therefore, has close affinities with her idea of art; in fact, as the discussion of her essays has suggested (chapter 2), life *is* art. "Form, as an element of human experience, must begin with the perception of separateness," she writes in her "Notes on Form in Art" (1868). Separateness, difference, necessarily precedes unity since what does not differ cannot be joined. It is true of life and art alike that "every difference is form." True, there are risks in emphasizing differences because some of them are not reconcilable in immediate or satisfactory ways. But this risk notwithstanding, George Eliot commends to her readers the double action of differentiation and unification, of sympathy and self-expression as the supremely moral act.

Romola

Romola (1863) is set in fifteenth-century Florence during a crucial period of transition between feudal and modern society. In her extensive research on Renaissance Florentine culture George Eliot attended to every feature of its life, its manners, its customs and slang, its dress, its religious and political and artistic developments. She made two trips to Italy for these investigations and kept notebook records of everything from theological doctrine to domestic detail. Sometimes this preparation seems to interfere with the naturalness of the descriptions, the contrivances sounding rather too audibly in the background. But by far the most common effect of this novel—an effect intensified by rereadings—is one of breathtaking audacity in both scope and conception. The metamorphoses of the Proem introduce a novel of extraordinary philosophical resonance and range. George Eliot's powerful grasp of the psychological corollaries of political traditions, the knowledge that supports her association of liberal traditions with humanist learning, her investigation of the dangerous gaps between intention and act—such interests make *Romola* one of George Eliot's most intriguing novels. Years after its publication she wrote to her editor, "there is no book of mine about which I more thoroughly feel that I could swear by every sentence as having been written with my best blood, such as it is, and with the most ardent care for veracity of which my nature is capable."[6]

The circumstances of its publication may account in part for the difference most readers feel between this work and her others. Of all her novels only *Romola* was not published by John Blackwood and only *Romola* was published serially. Her next novel, like her first two, was published complete and she published her last two novels each in eight parts. But when *Cornhill Magazine* published *Romola* it came out in fourteen monthly installments, each one composed of five chapters. As usual George Eliot had finished the plot outline before she began writing so she had her entire work in mind from the first; and during publication she kept about three installments (i.e., fifteen chapters) ahead of herself. But the circumstances of serial publication meant that she began publishing *Romola* before she finished writing it and for a novelist so scrupulous about form this must have made a difference. Dickens was a master at writing for serial publication and his event-filled, suspense-oriented novels seemed to thrive in it. But for George Eliot this format may well have committed her to print too early to allow for the reflectiveness generally characteristic of her work.

Romola's private story concerns the disillusionment of an idealistic girl. The crises of this personal history, however, stem from political developments in a turbulent period of Florentine history. George Eliot shows how the public struggle between political and religious authority reaches into the private history of her heroine. The man Romola marries, Tito Melema, a stranger in the city, insinuates himself into various positions by making himself useful, first to Romola's father, Bardo, a well-born scholar, and then to various factions vying for political power. Tito has betrayed his adoptive father, a scholar who was held for ransom and whom Tito abandoned to slavery, preferring the money to the parent. No sooner does he arrive in Medicean Florence than he sets up as a power-broker, intriguing among the various factions of that city-state. Tito, the complete political functionary, consults nothing but his own self-interest and the results do not recommend his procedure. On the unenlightened nature of Tito's self-promotion, the following comment is telling especially because it comes from a historical personage who occasionally appears in the margins of the story and who cannot be faulted for dreamy idealism. " 'It is a pity his falsehoods were not all of a wise sort,' said Machiavelli, with a melancholy shrug. 'With the times so much on his side as they are about church affairs, he might have done something great.' "[7] Tito makes betrayal a profession—first his adoptive father, then his father-in-law, then his wife, then even more powerful men, and finally himself.

Tito's undoing lies in a kind of self-betrayal that intrigues George Eliot. He cannot trust others, it is clear, because he cannot trust himself; consequently no one can trust him. Circumstances often catch Tito by surprise because he consults not circumstances but his own inclinations, and inclinations turn out to be inadequate guides to action. He shifts allegiance from one political faction to another until he is trusted by none—not because the politics of Medicean Florence are so pure but because his own lawlessness becomes increasingly evident. At one crisis, "he was at one of those lawless moments which come to us all if we have no guide but desire, and the pathway where desire leads us seems suddenly closed; he was ready to follow any beckoning that offered him an immediate purpose" (p.135; ch.13). George Eliot traces this weakness directly back to his inability to question himself. "It belongs to every large nature, when it is not under the immediate power of some strong unquestioning emotion, to suspect itself, and doubt the truth of its own impressions, conscious of possibilities beyond its own horizon" (p. 328; ch. 38). This description would serve as a good definition of sympathy as George Eliot understands it. Wholly absorbed in his plans for personal success, Tito lacks that capacity to see choices that would enable him to take the necessary risks for success. Confronted with an opportunity to save his benefactor from slavery he has one "colloquy with himself" but his love of ease triumphs. Tito does not act, under the impression that he is doing nothing, and "the little rills of selfishness" that had formerly been scattered "united and made a channel, so that they could never again meet with the same resistance" (p. 99; ch. 9): a splendid case of the banality of evil. In Tito, George Eliot gives a brilliant portrait of the circumstantial man: his secretiveness, his urge to be "safe," his instinct for mastery, and ultimately his self-destruction.

Despite her difficulties, despite her faltering, Romola has what Tito lacks: the power to question herself, the ability to acknowledge mistakes, and the capacity to recognize validity in claims inconsistent with her own. These powers necessarily entail risks to her independence. Alternatively submissive and rebellious, Romola seems to vacillate continuously without finding a way of her own. Her two flights into exile and her two returns dramatize in an extreme form her need for a center of self equivalent to those around her. When she flares up at Tito for having betrayed her dead father's trust by selling his unique library, she expresses her self-abnegation: "What else did I live for but for him and you?" (p. 280; ch. 32). With nothing to live for but two self-absorbed men, Romola first submits to them wholly and then, when they inevitably fail her ideal of them, she runs away. Locking away the symbols of her marriage she rebels against her life and sets out to begin a "new life," one of "loneliness and endurance, but of freedom." Once on the road she feels "free and alone" (pp. 322–23; ch. 37). Because she has confused submission with sympathy Romola finds her personal resources diminished by her efforts, and so attempts to find freedom in solitude. But in her act of flight the controversial religious leader Savonarola stops her and turns her back to a life of duty. " 'Live for Florence' " is his advice, and Romola submits again. " 'Father, I will be guided,' " she says reverentially, and "almost unconsciously she sank on her knees" (p. 355; ch. 40). Romola, like Maggie Tulliver, understands the importance of trusting others; she also likes to submit.

For a while she maintains this "enthusiasm of sympathy with the general life"—a very abstract form of sympathy—because she trusts to Savonarola's guidance. Eventually he, too, betrays her absolute trust, allowing Romola's godfather, an innocent man, to go to the scaffold for the sake of political expediency. When Romola appeals to him to put God's justice over the claims of party, Savonarola replies "the cause of my party *is* is the cause of God's kingdom." "I do not believe it!" Romola protests. "The two faces were lit up, each with an opposite certitude" (pp. 478–80; ch. 59). The claim of each is partially valid, yet the greater mistake clearly lies in Savonarola's sacrifice of human considerations for his view of superhuman ones. Whatever his provocations—and they are many—Savonarola's association of one ideology with Truth is a position that, in George Eliot's work, verges on blasphemy. Even one unbeliever, one individual with a different view qualifies the absolute claim of any position, and perhaps especially a position claiming God as an ally.

Once again Romola runs from conflict. This time she knows submission can never again be an option—"all clinging was at an end for her" (p. 486; ch. 60)—but she still confuses "clinging" with any social contact and gives both up together. This time no one turns her back and she discovers next that giving up on others means giving up on herself as well. "She was alone now: she had freed herself from all claims" and from saving occupation as well. "Romola felt orphaned in those wide spaces of sea and sky. She read no message of love for her in that far-off symbolic writing of the heavens, and with a great sob she wished that she might be gliding into death" (pp. 489–91; ch. 61). She has confused resignation with submission and she has confused activity with rebellion. Accident saves her from this confusion but not before she feels the deadly threat of total solitude. Neither in society nor in solitude does she find it possible to live.

And yet she does live. The process of vacillation itself produces growth and change in Romola. Precisely because she can vacillate between commitment and isolation Romola learns how to trust herself and how to find a center of self that makes possible engagement with others. In her efforts to escape commitment Romola resembles Tito to the extent that she confuses being "free" with being "alone." The hard lesson, the one Tito never learns, is that personal freedom can be found only in relation to others and not in opposition to them or in isolation from them.

Rebellion and submission are two sides of the same coin, both in personal relationships and in politics more broadly conceived. Romola's confusion as she vacillates between self-assertion and self-suppression at least maintains the conditions of growth whereas Tito's single-minded self-interest does not. The ability to accommodate views different from her own gives Romola her strength and it is in distinction from those views, in dialogue with those alter egos, that she finds her own view and her own voice. Without her own voice she pursues a kind of abstract, altruistic zeal, unchecked by feeling and experience. Romola's story confirms a Feuerbachian view of human possibility. The Christian pilgrim would find a message of love in the sky, but Romola only finds such answering messages in human society.

Silas Marner

When George Eliot made the first of her two Italian journeys she did some of the preparatory research for *Romola*; however, the fruit of this first journey was not *Romola* but a shorter tale called *Silas Marner*, which she published in 1861. It was, as she wrote Charles Bray, "quite a sudden inspiration that came across me in the midst of altogether different meditations." In her journal she describes it as a story that "has thrust itself between me and the other book I was meditating."[8] This elegant little tale, sometimes inflicted upon school children too young to grasp its depth, has more to it than an obvious moral about the superiority of love to money. An extended reflection on the problem of relationship, *Silas Marner* tells a double story about isolation and community.

The plot connects two separate stories, that of Silas Marner and that of Godfrey Cass, and within each story a problem exists about connection between past and present and consequently, between the central character and others. In Silas's story the central problem of community begins with betrayal. A member of a narrow religious sect in an industrial city, Silas resembles his brethren in almost everything, except in one particular—his tendency to fall into cataleptic trances. These "fits" the brethren accept sympathetically as Silas's unique gift until his best friend turns the gift against him. Disillusioned by this betrayal, Silas withdraws from Lantern Yard and from society almost altogether, moving to Raveloe, where he knows no one and where he can weave at his loom, hoard his earnings, and forget his past. George Eliot describes this retreat with metaphors of isolating enclosure. The sect of Latern Yard is a "little hidden world" withdrawn from the city and world affairs. From this Silas withdraws to his "hard isolation" in Raveloe, a place "hidden from the heavens."[9] Inside his isolated cottage Silas hides from his neighbors, and under his floor in a hole he hides his growing hoard of gold. His only gestures of affectionate response are made toward this gold, the product of his own activity. Like an insect spinning its means out of itself, with only the slenderest connection to the surrounding world and with only the slenderest nourishment, Silas regresses to the margins of humanity, his best faculties dormant for lack of exercise.

Counterpointing these metaphors of enclosure are metaphors of mysterious openings and of thresholds: the threshold between Silas and his neighbors, which few ever pass; the threshold between past and present, which Silas himself avoids crossing; and the threshold of consciousness represented by his cataleptic trances. In crossing these thresholds Silas begins the labor of reviving his connections to humanity. He begins directly after yet another betrayal, one to which even his minimal needs leave him vulnerable. One night, when he has left the cottage momentarily for water, a thief steals the unguarded gold, violating the secret life and forcing Silas into company.

Formerly, his heart had been as a locked casket with its treasure inside; but now the casket was empty, and the lock was utterly broken. Left groping in darkness, with his prop utterly gone, Silas had inevitably a sense, though a dull and half-despairing one, that if any help came to him it must come from without; and there was a slight stirring of expectation at the sight of his fellow-men, a faint consciousness of dependence on their good-will. He opened the door wide to admit Dolly. (p. 84; ch. 10)

The half-open door that offers admittance both to providers and to thieves emblematizes the risk and the opportunity of such openness, the need to control it, and the importance of that threshold between the private security and the public circumstance.

Silas's trances function for good and ill in a similarly ambiguous way. He is standing at his cottage door one night, handle in hand, when a fit overtakes him and, as he momentarily departs from consciousness into some other state, a child crawls past him through the half-open door. The special gift that was once an occasion for betrayal now proves a mysterious opening into a new life. The remainder of Silas's story mainly concerns his difficulties in raising the child, whom he calls Eppie, and the necessity, brought on him by her surprising infant habits, for more recourse to his neighbors for advice.

Meanwhile, the tale of Godfrey Cass concerns a different kind of tension between a man and his community. Godfrey's heart is divided between his established role as landowner and bachelor, and the secret life that has already made him a husband and father. Like the locked casket and the closed heart of Silas Marner, the sealed lips of Godfrey Cass isolate him and cut him off from nourishment. The barrenness of his second marriage particularly embitters him because he has left his own child unclaimed. The kinship that Godfrey secretly renounces Silas takes up, unknowingly replacing Godfrey as the father of the apparently orphaned infant. Secrets eventually come to light in George Eliot's fiction, through the intricate weblike interrelations of social life, and the plot concerns the nature and consequences of this secret's eventual revelation.

The patterns of similarity and difference between these two stories have enormous richness and complexity only suggested by this brief sketch of them. The relation of these plots has been developed elsewhere; what deserves notice here is the importance of this story in George Eliot's development. Her most mature work characteristically directs our attention to the points of contact between people who are only casually related. The development in *Silas Marner* of two apparently separate stories to a point of accidental connection anticipates the last novels. The central characters in *Silas* are linked not by blood ties or legal ties, as they are in the first two novels, but by accidents of neighborhood, accidents that become important at critical moments in *Romola* and in *Felix Holt* and that become continuously important in *Middlemarch* and in *Daniel Deronda*. The mutual dependence of strangers comes home in this short tale as it has not formerly in the novels and introduces a theme central to the form of George Eliot's greatest work.

The reader sees influence between strangers clearly in this tale, even though the characters themselves make little of it. By focusing on the covergence of separate histories George Eliot emphasizes the importance of trust in dealing with conflicting claims. To perceive another's opposition as a resource requires, as Romola's experience demonstrates, a certain strength of character. Romola's trust in Tito makes her vulnerable to bitter disappointment; she finally despairs of her marriage when she realizes that there is a "terrible flaw in the trust." Silas's "trusting simplicity" likewise makes him vulnerable to a rapacious friend (p. 11; ch. 1). But while trust creates vulnerability it also binds these characters to life and change in spite of their efforts to escape. The homely wisdom of Dolly Winthrop puts it to Silas directly. "If anything looks hard to me, it's because there's things I don't know on; and, for the matter o' that, there may be plenty o' things I don't know on, for its little I know—that it is. . . . And all as we've got to do is to trusten, Master Marner—to do the right things as fur as we know and to trusten" (p. 149; ch. 16). The matter of "right" and "wrong" here become tolerably confused, as it should in a universe with few moral absolutes. Dolly's advice puts in simple terms the negative capability that for George Eliot makes sympathy possible. The "right" of any view is always qualified, used in a hypothetical way, understood in practical not dogmatic terms.

What comes gradually to Romola and Silas is a kind of resignation that is the opposite of losing the self. By acknowledging the difference between themselves and others, by accepting the gaps between their desires and their abilities, they both validate their individual experience and locate it in relation to others. "What if," Romola reflects, "What if the life of Florence was a web of inconsistencies? Was she, then, something higher, that she should shake the dust from off her feet, and say 'This world is not good enough for me?' If she had really been higher, she would not so easily have lost all her trust" (p. 547; ch. 69). The ability to sustain conflict without irritability reaching for certainty holds open the possibility for change and growth. A character in *Middlemarch* sums up the proper attitude best. "I have not given up doing as I like, but I can very seldom do it." [10]

Without sympathy and trust in the possibilities of others, characters like Godfrey Cass and Tito demonstrate the alternative experience of enmity and suspicion. Hostage to their secrets these characters remain alone even in company. They remain on guard, defensive, fearful of discovery when discovery alone would save them. One of George Eliot's favorite metaphors for this destructive instinct is gambling. The metaphor first appears clearly developed in *Silas Marner* and it reappears with special definition in *Felix Holt* and in *Daniel Deronda*. Often associated with cramped spaces and with narcotic influences, gambling is a kind of unholy opposite to sympathetic relationships because it pits individuals against each other and reduces the importance of their personal, individualizing differences. For example, *Daniel Deronda* opens at the roulette table in a continental gambling casino, with an international company:

Livonian and Spanish, Graeco-Italian and miscellaneous German, English aristocratic and English plebian. Here certainly was a striking admission of human equality. . . . Where else would her ladyship have graciously consented to sit by that dry-lipped feminine figure prematurely old, withered after short bloom like her artificial flowers, holding a shabby velvet reticule before her, and occasionally putting in her mouth the point with which she pricked her card?

The atmosphere of "dull gas-poisoned absorption" suspends spontaneous activity and personal differences for the sake of the mechanical wheel. " 'Faites votre jeu, mesdames et messieurs,' said the automatic voice of destiny." [11] The "uniform negativeness" of the players' expressions has the "effect of a mask," reducing to monotonous likeness all the differences implied by the description. *Silas Marner* anticipates the last novel in several ways, and most strikingly in its attention to this metaphor.

Silas's history, too, opens with a form of gambling, one literally elevated into a religious program. The worshippers of Lantern Yard venerate "favorable chance," also the god of Godfrey (God-free) Cass and "of all men who follow their own devices instead of obeying a law they believe in" (p. 77; ch. 9). These worshippers actually gamble for salvation by putting moral questions to a lottery. In Silas's case the lottery decides the guilt of an innocent man and benefits his betrayer. Gamblers, these and others, rely on chance to protect them from ordinary probabilities and to fulfill their desires by some magic. This converts life into "a hideous lottery, where every day may turn up a blank." [12] Mrs. Transome in *Felix Holt,* of whom this observation is made, is one of George Eliot's losing gamblers. Without abandoning her establishment Mrs. Transome attempts to live apart from the codes and obligations of her society, as if she could escape by an act of will from any hindrance to her inclination. The novel dramatizes the consequences. "There is no private life," says the narrator of *Felix Holt,* "which has not been determined by a wider public life, from the time when the primeval milkmaid had to wander with the wanderings of her clan, because the cow she milked was one of a herd which had made the pastures bare" (p. 51; ch. 3). Ignoring the determinate givens of experience is the most desperate gamble because it involves a withdrawal from opportunity as well as from limitation.

Felix Holt

In *Felix Holt, the Radical* (1866) George Eliot considers the social "web of inconsistencies" in a way that consolidates the gains she made in *Silas Marner* and shifts the balance in her fiction toward a new focus of attention. Like the novel preceding it, *Felix Holt* sets a courtship and marriage against a background of political and legal affairs, this time the affairs of England just preceding the Reform Act of 1832. But neither the private history of Esther Lyons's marriage to Felix Holt nor the public life represented by politics and legalities holds center stage in this novel. *Felix Holt* magnifies the pattern found in *Silas Marner* of accidental conjunction between separate groups. Such meetings between plots become the center of attention: not merely the relations within families nor the relations between one family and general social background, but rather the relations between families. In previous novels there is an important gap between the world of strangers and the world of friends and the action takes place in a foreground of personal interest set against a background of public concern. In *Felix Holt* the background *is* the foreground. In all her novels George Eliot shows a special capacity to imagine these connections between private and public, between the momentary inclination and social institutions. In *Felix Holt* she diversifies the center of private interest and so brings into relief the problems of negotiation between them.

This novel traces the "mutual influence of dissimilar destinies" (p. 52; ch. 3), attending mainly to parallels between individuals who scarcely know each other. For example, both Felix Holt and Harold Transome declare themselves to be politically "radical." One is a

working man, the other heir to Transome Court, and they have little
in common either as radicals, or as sons and suitors. The novel's title
suggests with subtle irony the impossibility of "radical" change in a
world where complex circumstances condition every action. Careless
of this context, Harold trusts to his own skill "to shape the success
of his own morrows, ignorant of what many yesterdays had determined for him beforehand" (p. 186; ch. 16); and Felix, full of idealistic zeal, finds that his efforts have unpredictable consequences and
that support can come from unlikely quarters. In their different ways
both characters learn the hard way to respect the powerful web of circumstances; and through this network of circumstance "Felix Holt
made a considerable difference in the life of Harold Transome, though
nature and fortune seemed to have done what they could to keep the
lots of the two men quite aloof from each other" (p. 52; ch. 3).

The plot in *Felix Holt* operates at two levels, each strangely separate
from the other. On the one hand, there is the daily domestic contact
between individuals, on the other, the tangle of legal entails bearing
on these individuals, first secretly and then directly. The legal status
of the characters almost seems like a repressed part of their lives, rele-
gated by time and some strategic planning on the part of a few, to a
kind of shadow existence. This separation between the foreground and
background of the plot emphasizes how remarkably far-reaching are
the levels of disconnection in the society of Treby Magna. But the
assorted clues of the past are bound by a single secret that, when it
comes to light, brings with it a new, reordered social arrangement in
which Esther Lyon and Harold Transome play rather different parts
than those for which they had prepared themselves. Esther and
Harold are not who they think they are, socially or legally, and the
discovery of these ambiguities presses directly on their strength of
character as individuals. Esther discovers that the man she thought
was her father is really an adoptive father, and that the wealthy life
she has only dreamed about is actually her by inheritance. Poor
Harold discovers a series of false bottoms in his past that utterly con-
fuse his sense of who he is. He is a sort of fake-Transome because his
ancestors took over the name of another, degenerate family; worse, he
is not even a fake-Transome in actual parentage but secretly the son
of Matthew Jermyn, the man he most hates.

The central parallel in the novel lies between Esther Lyon, the
young woman with a future, and Mrs. Transome, the aging woman
with a past. Mrs. Transome is a sort of historical alter ego for Esther,

a possible version of herself; as such Mrs. Transome acts as an embodiment of one alternative about which Esther must choose when she decides whether to become mistress of Transome Court. As a girl Mrs. Transome trifled away her intelligence in being clever and in trying to "rule"; she loved elegance, gaiety, and above all the admiration of men. These are the very qualities in Esther that Felix rudely challenges. Like Mrs. Transome in her youth, Esther loves French romantic novels, has contempt for Wordsworth, imagines an imperial future in which she will move in a starring role through life, and loves chivalry in men. She likes to "rule" and, despite Felix's ridicule, thinks of power in terms of sexual politics, romantically conceived. For example, Esther "was fond of netting, because it showed to advantage both her hand and her foot; and across this image of Felix Holt's indifference and contempt there passed the vaguer image of a possible somebody who would admire her hands and feet, and delight in looking at their beauty, and long, yet not dare, to kiss them" (p. 174; ch. 15).

Harold Transome actually materializes, like an answer to a careless prayer, to fulfill this daydream: chivalrous, condescending, polite, kind. He arrives in England from a life in the Far East where he married and lost a wife. He treats his son with good intentions but as part of the baggage. He has not known Esther a week when "he had made up his mind to marry her; and it had never entered into that mind that the decision did not rest entirely with his inclination" (p. 380; ch. 60). Soon after Miss Lyon has occasion to exclaim of this paragon:

"How chivalrous you are!" said Esther, as Harold, kneeling on one knee, held her silken netting-stirrup for her to put her foot through. She had often fancied pleasant scenes in which such homage was rendered to her, and the homage was not disagreeable now it was really come; but, strangely enough, a little darting sensation at that moment was accompanied by the vivid remembrance of someone who had never paid the least attention to her foot.

Harold elaborates "A woman ought never to have any trouble. There should always be a man to guard her from it" (382–83). This kind of protection, carelessly offered on an assumption of superior mastery, resembles the "protection" of the kind extortionists impose upon their victims. The ominousness of his remark is clearest in context of his behavior to his mother and of her former lover's behavior to her.

Mrs. Transome's history is a "parable" of violence, of an "under-world" with "thorn-bushes," and "thick-barked stems" that "have human histories hidden in them; the power of unuttered cries dwells in the passionless-seeming branches, and the red warm blood is darkly feeding the quivering nerves of a sleepless memory that watches through all dreams" (p. 11; introduction). The contrast between Esther's fantasies and this realization in Mrs. Transome link the two characters and link the fantasy with its terrible consequences.

The politics of homage in domestic life resemble the politics of dominance and submission characteristic of the traditional political system forming the context for *Felix Holt's* romantic plot. The traditional governance by hierarchies based on inherited rank conflicts with the emerging politics of consensus for which Felix Holt campaigns. This connection between private habits and public systems is one of this novel's most striking accomplishments.

In contrast to Esther's encounter with Harold in the scene just quoted, this scene with Felix establishes among other things the difference in tone and quality between the two relationships. I quote at length to catch the poise and mobility of this psychological exchange. Felix, according to his custom with Esther, begins chastizing her for spending time on "trifles," in particular romantic novels.

"You are kind enough to say so. But I am not aware that I have ever confided my reasons to you."

"Why what worth calling a reason could make any mortal hang over this trash?—idiotic immorality dressed up to look fine, with a little bit of doctrine tacked to it, like a hare's foot. . . . Look here! 'Est-ce ma faute, si je trouve partout les bornes, si ce qui est fini n'a pour moi aucune valeur?' ['Is it my fault, if I find limits everywhere, if what is completed has no value for me?'] Yes, sir, distinctly your fault, because you're an ass. Your dunce who can't do his sums always has a taste for the infinite. . . ."

"Oh pray, Mr. Holt, don't go on reading with that dreadful accent; it set's one's teeth on edge." Esther, smarting helplessly under the previous lashes, was relieved by this diversion of criticism.

"There it is!" said Felix, throwing the book on the table, and getting up to walk about. "You are only happy when you can spy a tag or a tassel loose to turn the talk, and get rid of any judgment that must carry grave action after it. . . . I can't bear to see you going the way of the foolish women who spoil men's lives. . . . I'll never love, if I can help it; and if I love, I'll bear it, and never marry. . . ."

"I ought to be very much obliged to you for giving me your confidence so freely."

"Ah! Now you are offended with me, and disgusted with me. I expected it would be so. A woman doesn't like a man who tells her the truth."

"I think you boast a little too much of your truth-telling, Mr. Holt," said Esther, flashing out at last. "That virtue is apt to be easy to people when they only wound others and not themselves. Telling the truth often means no more than taking a liberty."

"Yes, I suppose I should have been taking a liberty if I had tried to drag you back by the skirt when I saw you running into a pit."

"You really should found a sect. Preaching is your vocation. It is a pity you should ever have an audience of only one."

"I see; I have made a fool of myself. I thought you had a more generous mind—that you might be kindled to a better ambition. But I've set your vanity aflame—nothing else. I'm going. Good-by." (pp. 126–28; ch. 10)

This skirmish could not differ more from the genteel flirtation between Esther and Harold. There each retains privately an agenda that conflicts with the other (each intends to rule). There the opposition is unstated and so remains divisive. But here the differences acknowledged provide a basis for sympathetic understanding. Not agreement, not compromise, but clear difference of the sort that escalates irritation into anger, that leads people to overstate what they mean, that eventually ends like Romola's argument with Savonarola unsatisfactorily for both; and yet a difference that forms the basis for a relationship, literally an engagement by the end. Felix is partly right and partly foolish (I'll never love, if I can help it; and if I love, I'll bear it, and never marry"); Esther is partly foolish in her tastes and partly right in her fury at Felix's impertinence ("You really should found a sect"). Nobody here makes an absolute claim so nobody forecloses the connection. Here the conflict of valid claims, partly thanks to the relatively trivial stakes, shows it creative possibility. Esther's running battle with Felix differs considerably from the cold oppositions between Mrs. Transome and her men. Opposition makes Mrs. Transome afraid, it stimulates Esther's intelligence and anger.

Beyond these comparisons, this conversation also reveals something new, a fuller sense of tension *within* individuals, a sense of the gap between outward gesture and inner consciousness. There is nothing like it in *Adam Bede* or *Silas Marner* and little in *The Mill on the Floss* or *Romola*. In *Adam Bede*, for example, Dinah Morris and Adam experience their conflicts between inclination and duty in less subtle and internal ways. Dinah seems to live comfortably enough without much private life and then, after she meets Adam, she chooses to get happily married. Though the narrator tells us of her private turmoil we are not made to feel the struggle. By comparison with Arthur Donnithorne's emotional journey hers seems very deliberate and clear. Adam undergoes his dark night of the soul with similar deliberateness. They both seem to know where they are, however problematic their situation may be. Dinah always speaks in the same calm voice, whether she is speaking to Seth, or Hetty, or a congregation, or herself. The sense of distinction between private and public life, the sense of faceted consciousness and inward tension simply does not blur Dinah's clarity. She knows how to choose. This, too, is a human possibility, one George Eliot associates with a traditional social structure or with Evangelicalism's best influence. But these supports to psychic life are failing even in the first novel and unavailable in the last; and as they fade, the importance of exchange between individuals increases. Clarity of self-definition depends upon the contact with others; in Feuerbachian terms, the "I" depends upon exchange with "Thou." In the exchange between Felix and Esther, for example, there is more irony, more self-consciousness than there was between Dinah and Adam, between Maggie and Stephen.

The mutual influence of dissimilar destinies spreads wide in *Felix Holt*, beyond a group of families or a neighborhood to a national life on the brink of structural change. This historical moment, that of the Reform Bills, appears only in the margins but acts to extend the sense of connection between widely separated lives. Like the activity of the narrator and the artist discussed in preceding chapters, this introduction of a wider social life requires the reader to recognize distinctions and to make connections where the characters often do not. This activity is as central to sympathy as sympathy is to moral life and as both are to aesthetic activity: all depend upon that ability to make connections which follows from the ability to perceive difference or separation.

Chapter Five
Secrecy and Confession: *Middlemarch* and *Daniel Deronda*

The connection between private and public life remains one of George Eliot's constant themes from the beginning of her work to the end. For her, however, privacy belongs by definition to a thoroughly public conception of human circumstances and is not to be confused with secrecy, a disorder that cripples both private and public life by introducing into individual consciousness a dissociation between thought and action. Facing the inevitable conflicts of life, for example, Arthur Donnithorne attempts to avoid choice by thinking one thing and doing another. By separating thought and action he attempts to lead a double life rather than to admit plainly, either to himself or, if necessary, to another, the existence of those conflicts that prepare for him inevitable choices. Such dissociation can be healed only by the reunion of thought and action that comes with such admission, often called "confession" in the novels.

The problem of secrecy, most important in *Middlemarch*, is one that plagues characters from *Adam Bede* on, and it is an individual problem with public consequences. Arthur Donnithorne keeps half his mind secret from himself and so it cannot be grasped by others. Like Arthur, Tito Melema knows the whole truth about himself, but only some of the time. The power of secrecy permits such men to postpone their reckonings until they have passed a point of no return. Godfrey Cass keeps his secret for sixteen years, resisting the sense of compunction so evident by contrast in Silas Marner's confession to his neighbor Jem Rodney; and the cost to Godfrey is the loss of his daughter to Silas. In Arthur, Tito, Hetty, Godfrey, Mrs. Transome, and other like them, the resistance to the sense of compunction is what hardens their self-division and puts self-control out of their reach. In *Middlemarch* the problems of secrecy are multiplied, especially in the histories of three professional men. In her portraits of Casaubon, Bulstrode, and Lydgate—scholar, banker, and doctor— George Eliot shows the unremitting blight that secrecy casts over each of their lives. Their lack of candor, though similar to Arthur Donnithorne's in a simpler society, clearly flourishes more easily in a more complex and densely populated environment like that of Middlemarch.

Where *Middlemarch* traces the dissociation of thought and action through secrecy, *Daniel Deronda* traces the reunion of thought and action in the act of confession. Confession, too, is a constant theme in the novels, all of which stress the importance of telling the truth to ing one's secret, is an act that inevitably punctures the fear that prompts secrecy and obliterates the futile wish that facts can be eluded or ignored. But such confession to oneself is also demonstrably difficult when the inner conscience is weak. The power of confession lies in trust, and if not of oneself, then of another, who acts as a kind of external conscience, reinforcing the weak internal one and strengthening its resolve. By admitting to another what one is reluctant to admit to oneself, "the hope in lies is forever swept away."[1] Once the secret has been confessed to another person, more than one person has to be fooled, and when another consciousness is involved with one's own, the conditions of personal choice are changed. Hetty Sorrel is the one most in need of the admission she finally makes to Dinah Morris; everyone else already has most of the information she still denies until that moment. This moment of confession is unique and isolated in other novels but in *Daniel Deronda* the act of confession is repeated and is the central link between the two distinct plots. Through an act of trust between two relative strangers, Gwendolen Harleth and Daniel Deronda, the woman with a secret history and the man who reluctantly becomes her temporary benefactor, the deep divisions in this novel are bridged.

Though secrecy and confession appear in all George Eliot's fiction, the context for them changes in the last two novels. From the domestic or community circles of early works George Eliot has moved to interdomestic and even international networks of influence. Where the first four novels focus on relationships between members of a family or clan, or within a single community, *Middlemarch* and *Daniel Deronda* focus on relationships between more casual acquaintances or even between relative strangers. The context of pluralistic possibilities that is always present in the margins of her plots receives fullest for-

mal representation in these last two. Where *Adam Bede* focuses on
four households, *Middlemarch* focuses on at least ten, and *Daniel Deronda* has equal plot diversity with, in addition, a cultural range new
in her fiction, including different national and cultural traditions. As
the range of representation widens, the plots change their emphasis,
moving from complications that find resolution in marriage, that is,
in an incorporation of intimacy, to complications that do not find resolution and that involve other forms of intimacy than marriage. The
central constructive relationships in both novels are between friends,
and most central in each case is the friendship between a man and a
woman.

Middlemarch

Middlemarch, published in a new, eight-part format in 1872, out-
stripped even *Adam Bede* in popularity. The plot nearly defies summary. Its action radiates from various centers of activity outward in a
vast network of influence where one plot echoes another, distinctly
and yet with an incompleteness sufficient to cancel any easy generalizations about meaning. Many of the crucial moments in the novel
concern the inward divisions in each of the three men already mentioned, Dorothea's first husband, Edward Casaubon, the idealistic
doctor Tertius Lydgate who has an unfortunate weakness for pretty
faces, and the pious banker Nicholas Bulstrode. Each is only casually
acquainted with himself. Each uses his professional ambition as an excuse for human coarseness and omission. Each relies on secrecy, either
from others or from himself, as a means of gaining power or control.
And each finds out too late that this resort to secrecy is inadequate
and self-destructive. George Eliot traces in their histories the moments of decision, enacted and then reenacted until a reflex and then
a habit is formed that paralyzes their powers of sympathy and eventually proves destructive of their own most cherished ambitions. The
successes in personal mastery on the other hand, such as Dorothea's
or Camden Farebrother's or Caleb Garth's, provide important relief
from these central histories of defeat. *Middlemarch* is a thoroughly
amusing novel; the narrator is never more charming and the characters' disappointments never more justified. But it is a serious novel
and demanding in its attention to the real psychic maneuvers of actual
men and women. It is probably this mature quality of its attention
that prompted Virginia Woolf to make the remark by now so often

quoted that *Middlemarch* was the first English novel written for grown-ups.[2] Though it begins and ends with the delightful Miss Brooke, the center stage in *Middlemarch* is occupied with the failures of private confession, that is, the failures to admit one's own actual motives and the reliance on secrecy in order to function socially.

Book 1, "Miss Brooke," introduces Dorothea and her sister Celia, both orphans living with their amiable, muddle-headed uncle, Mr. Brooke. The focus of this book, until its last chapter, is Dorothea's shortsighted engagement to Edward Casaubon, a man more than twice her age, and a learned but pedantic scholar. Nearly all other main characters are introduced in connection with Dorothea's engagement, although many await development in later books. These include (besides the three men already mentioned) the Vincy family, composed of the mercantile Mr. Vincy and his mercenary wife and children, Rosamond and Fred; Sir James Chettham, who courts the eldest Miss Brooke until she chooses another and then turns to her sister; Mrs. Cadwallader, the town diplomatist, and her clergyman husband, a man more interested in fishing than in his flock; and various miscellaneous characters from the gentry and professional classes of Middlemarch invited to celebrate Dorothea's improbable marriage. The main characters absent from this group for reasons of occupation or disposition are Caleb Garth and his plain, agreeable family, all people with more sense than money; and the disagreeable master of Stone Court, the ailing Peter Featherstone, who has more money than sense and who is locked in mutual hostility with his ever-watchful heirs.

This first book, like the others, is punctuated by public events that bring people together more or less casually—engagements and weddings, funerals, business meetings, taverns, New Year's parties. At these moments the private histories of one family or another open upon each other with mutual and unexpected influence: influence not of an extreme or especially noticeable kind, but influence nonetheless that weighs in the balance of actions done or not done, decisions taken or avoided. The remaining seven books develop themes initiated in this one. Their titles suggest one way George Eliot draws parallels between separate histories: "Old and Young" (book 2), "Waiting for Death" (book 3), "Three Love Problems" (book 4), "The Dead Hand" (book 5), "Widow and Wife" (book 6), "Two Temptations" (book 7), and "Sunset and Sunrise" (book 8). Each book quietly insists on the common ground of separate lives by forcing us to shift our attention from one history to another, and to attend to the importance of ordinary moments. "Old and Young," for example, compares old medical ideas with those new ones introduced by the young Lydgate; it compares the sensibility of the old Casaubon with that of his young wife; and it compares the young hopes of Fred Vincy and Mary Garth with the miserliness of old Featherstone, her employer and his potential benefactor. The connections between them are arbitrary to an extent, and yet based in a matrix of common experience. In book 3, death no sooner takes Peter Featherstone, leaving behind a hoard of disappointed relatives, than its specter begins hovering at Lowick over Casaubon; his "Dead Hand" (book 5) holds onto Dorothea's life through his crabbed will, while an old acquaintance of Bulstrodes' returns to renew a death-grip on his life. Book 6 compares Dorothea and Rosamond as "Widow and Wife," expecially as regards their sense of purpose and their influence on others. Book 7 treats the "Two Temptations" of Farebrother and of Bulstrode, a comparison that underscores the radically different consequences of a life of secrecy, like Bulstrode's, from those consequences of the habitual self-knowledge demonstrated in Farebrother's crucial confession. "Sunset and Sunrise" (book 8) parallels the eclipse of Lydgate's bright hopes with the emergence of Dorothea's hard-won new life. The arbitrariness of the connections suggested by the book titles corresponds to the clear sense in this novel that individual awareness must always deal with a world it has not made. What seems unique to an individual is not unique but a common structure of experience. Isolation is impossible, and the secretive attempt to remain apart a delusive, doomed effort.

Of the principal histories in *Middlemarch*, only one is the story of a success. Where Casaubon, Bulstrode, and Lydgate fail to make important admissions to themselves, Dorothea Brooke succeeds, and her story frames the novel. Dorothea's secret from herself is that she has personal desires. How it is possible for someone to hide such a truth from herself is a question, and a measure of Dorothea's quixotic nature. Her mind is full of lofty conceptions for the benefit of her fellow creatures. She "likes giving up" as her sister Celia complains, no doubt with a practical sense of irritation at being so often eclipsed in virtue.[3] The novel opens with a scene between the two in which they divide their mother's jewels, Dorothea secretly admiring their beauty and trying to renounce them as much as possible. Her fault is an excess of her virtue. She longs to be useful, to *do* something particular, to desire "what is perfectly good, even when we don't quite know what it is" (p. 287; ch. 39). But she is so bent on making other lives better, that she shirks her enjoyment of her own. "It spoils my enjoyment of anything when I am made to think that most people are shut out from it" (p. 163; ch. 22), she complains to Will Ladislaw. He is rightly appalled, calling that "the fanaticism of sympathy." Dorothea devotes herself to projects to combat her sense of uselessness. "She had been oppressed by the indefiniteness which hung in her mind, like a thick summer haze, over all her desire to make her life greatly effective. What could she do, what ought she to do?" (p. 20; ch. 3). Her female's education having left her with no vocation, she contents herself with making plans for laborer's cottages, until she lights upon Mr. Casaubon as the ideal sort of man for a husband, a kind of cross between a father and the poet, Milton, to whom she could be both pupil and assistant.

This marriage very soon reveals its shallowness to her, and she awakens from her ignorant illusion of her husband's great work at which she had thought to be a "lamp-holder." George Eliot's portrait of this marriage is relentless in its pursuit of the false consciousness in each, that prevents them from knowing one another in time. Only Casaubon's death frees her from burial in his fruitless, labyrinthine work and cold unresponsive personality. Her friendship with Casaubon's cousin, Will Ladislaw, on the other hand, is the sunny relationship of equals, a fact not lost on the jealous older man who leaves Dorothea compromised in his will. His money will be hers, he stipulates from beyond the grave, unless she marries Ladislaw. This thought of marriage to Ladislaw has never entered her mind, though it has seldom been far from Ladislaw's. Even when she has learned the full extent of her husband's deceitful nature, and the true worthlessness of his work, and even when she has learned that Ladislaw does love her, she permits herself to say good-bye to him without acknowledging mutual feeling and without thinking of giving up her husband's money for the sake of a new marriage. She is at her worst when, having just said goodbye to Ladislaw, she drives past him on the road in her carriage leaving him plodding in the dust, portionless and unable to declare himself as a candidate for her hand. Having made a miserable marriage out of falsely high-minded motives, she continues to leave herself out of the picture even when there appears to be no earthly reason for doing so.

Book 8 begins with Dorothea's "impetuous generosity" extending itself in a different direction, towards Lydgate, who has become falsely implicated in the seedy doings of Bulstrode. It is through this extension of herself that Dorothea, quite by accident, finally learns to know herself. In her willingness to aid him, she offers not only money but a visit of solace to his wife, Rosamond. The visit ends prematurely, however, when Dorothea discovers Ladislaw in what appears to be a compromising attitude, comforting the tearful Rosamond himself. She returns home, "the limit of endurance" reached after so much giving up, and in the dark night that follows she confesses to herself the feelings for Ladislaw that she has never before acknowledged. When she opens her curtains the next morning in a gesture of restoration to the world and its troubles, she does so with a new sense of her *own* troubles. The capacity finally to acknowledge her personal desires readies her to do what she has unaccountably not done before, give up her encumbered money and acknowledge her own transparent feelings for Will. It is the admission of *her* desire, *her* sorrow, *her* love and jealousy that must come before she can assert her personal claims. She returns to Rosamond, unwilling to leave her original purpose unachieved, but the prerequisite for her reunion with Ladislaw is her reunion with herself; Rosamond merely sets her straight concerning the true direction of Ladislaw's feeling. The extraordinary scene between the two women does not alter the essential character of either, but it does deflect the course of their inward awarenesses in ways that have lasting influence in both their lives.

The secrets of Casaubon, Bulstrode, and Lydgate do not have the same innocence as Dorothea's. Casaubon has made a profession of keeping secrets from himself. "All through his life Mr. Casaubon has been trying not to admit even to himself the inward sores of self-doubt and jealousy" that haunt his scholarship long before they haunt his marriage (p. 277; ch. 37). The Key to All Mythologies that he proposes to discover and then (having "once mastered the true position") to use for explaining the entire field of mythic constructions, is a work doomed by his inability to penetrate his vast material or to accept a provisional rather than "the true" conclusion. But his zeal for this project stems from other than scholarly motives. He has formulated his conception, not out of interest in life but out of competitive jealousy, and consequently nothing interferes with the unproductiveness of his effort. He marries Dorothea with the mistaken notion that he had found a submissive young admirer with no aim but that of serving his ambition. His mistake is soon as evident to him as Dorothea's is to her, but his reaction is rather different. Having formulated his life's aim in terms of competitive jealousy, Casaubon continues to explain his marital failures in a similar way. He suspects his innocent wife of betraying him with Ladislaw. "He suspected this, however, as he suspected other things, without confessing it, and like the rest of us, felt how soothing it would have been to have a companion who would never find it out." The more he retreats into proud reticence the more outrageous his fantasy of betrayal becomes. "To all the facts which he knew, he added imaginary facts both present and future which became more real to him than those, because they called up a stronger dislike, a more predominating bitterness" (p. 307; ch. 42). The net effect of his secretiveness is to undermine Dorothea's trust and veneration and, as he withdraws farther into false reasoning, to bury his conscience altogether and with it his reputation. When his will is read Dorothea learns from the codicil, enjoining her against marrying Ladislaw if she wishes to keep her property, that he has been all along petty and vengeful and "not like a gentleman" (p. 359, ch. 50). The "shock of revulsion from her departed husband, who had had hidden thoughts, perhaps perverting everything she said or did (360) chills any interest she may have had in loyally continuing his work. Casaubon thus achieves the very opposite of what he sought, revealing to his entire world the "hungry, shivering self" he bent a lifetime of effort to hide (p. 206; ch. 29).

By comparison with Casaubon, whose worst influence unfolds in his marriage, Nicholas Bulstrode's carefully maintained ignorance of himself directly injures many other people. We learn in flashbacks that Bulstrode's habits began forming in his youth when he was the pious member of a rigorous Protestant sect and already possessed of the conviction "that God intended him for special instrumentality." He recalls his own first shrinking when he is invited by a member of his congregation to fill a vacancy in the exceedingly profitable family business. "The business was a pawnbroker's" and the profits those available from "the easy reception of any goods offered, without strict inquiry as to where they came from." Somehow Brother Bulstrode's "shrinking remained private" and he found himself "carrying on two distinct lives," one as a pious pillar of the church and one as a fence for stolen goods. The first compromise taken, however, another becomes easier. When his partner dies and Bulstrode proposes to the widow, he learns that she wants first to locate her remaining child, a daughter who had fled in disgust from the family and had married abroad, perhaps having a child of her own. The daughter had been found, "but only one man besides Bulstrode knew it, and he was paid for keeping silence and carrying himself away" (pp. 451–52; ch. 61). The return of this man, John Raffles, after years threatens the respectability that Bulstrode, in a different town and with a different wife, has built on this secret past.

His behavior under this challenge proves that the man who profited from the betrayal of his friends, even by acts of omission and even years ago, is the same man who neglects, consciously and with malice, the single communication that will save his enemy's life. Alone in his house at midnight, the objectionable Raffles asleep under his care, and Lydgate departed after leaving his medical instructions, Bulstrode confronts the opportunity to let his housekeeper misapply medication. The quantity of "diseased motive" already present in Bulstrode relaxes his hold on truth. "His conscience was soothed by the enfolding wing of secrecy. . . . And who could say that the death of Raffles had been hastened? Who knew what would have saved him" (p. 521; ch. 70). Unaccustomed to choosing between conflicting desires, and accustomed to relying on secrecy to cover results he does not exert himself to hinder, Bulstrode finds himself at the mercy of his lies. In convincing himself effectively to murder Raffles so as to prevent him from talking, Bulstrode does not consider the possibility, indeed the probability that Raffles has already talked. But he has, and the town knows of the past alliance. When Raffles dies, rumor spreads and Bulstrode eventually faces, in the worst public humiliation, that voice of discipline he had not heeded in himself.

Lydgate is the most interesting character in *Middlemarch*, from the point of view of self-betrayal. Unlike Casaubon and Bulstrode who are past middle-age when we meet them, Lydgate is only twenty-seven and his character still in the making. He seems to have everything to recommend him—he is well born and has a small but independent income, he is dedicated to medical science and to research of a venturesome kind, he has the courage to differ from the quackery of his colleagues and the tact to respond to the needs of others; and yet be betrays himself into disappointment, shabby achievement, and he dies an early death. In chapter 15 the narrator sums up the analysis of his character and prospects as follows: "How could there be any commonness in a man so well-bred, so ambitious of social distinction, so generous and unusual in his views of social duty? . . . Lydgate's spots of commonness lay in the complexion of his prejudices . . . : that distinction of mind which belonged to his intellectual ardour, did not penetrate his feeling and judgment about furniture, or women, or the desirability of its being known (without his telling) that he was better born than other country surgeons." While "he did not mean to think of furniture at present," when he did so his furniture would naturally be the best (111–12). "As to women," the narrator immediately informs us, he was once drawn into an impetuous folly over an actress whom he knew nothing of. He pursues her and even proposes marriage, even though "he knew that this was like the sudden impulse of a madman. . . . No matter! . . . He had two selves within him apparently, and they must learn to accommodate each other" (113). Madame Laure's cool revelation of her character, quite a different one than the idealized version in Lydgate's imagination, appalls him, but spares him this time from making a fatal marriage. The conclusion of this episode leaves him with the romantic illusion "that illusions were at an end for him" (114). He does not inquire too closely about the two selves that act in conflict, or about the possibility that he might repeat such unexpected action against his own avowed intentions.

Lydgate's fatal sense of superiority to daily affairs, his restlessness with the "hampering, threadlike pressures" of everyday conditions, embroil him the more easily in engagements about which he has thought little. It is early evident that Rosamond Vincy has decided to marry him, and that she is wholly unsuitable to his proposed way of life and incapable of understanding his ambition. "It is true that Lydgate had the counter-idea of remaining unengaged; but this was a mere negative, a shadow cast by other resolves which themselves were capable of shrinking. Circumstance was almost sure to be on the side of Rosamond's idea, which had a shaping activity and looked through watchful blue eyes, whereas Lydgate's lay blind and unconcerned as a jelly-fish which gets melted without knowing it" (p. 200; ch. 27). Such language as this, repeatedly used to suggest the "torpedo contact" of Rosamond's determination, captures the primitive nature of the struggle between them, even though it takes place in the politeness of drawing room talk and without either of them ever understanding the other's intentions, or even, possibly, their own. It is no surprise to anyone but Lydgate, given the probabilities of his character, that he finds himself more often with Rosy than he intended; even when he senses her position and deliberately intends to avoid her, he is led to offer marriage almost carelessly, on the spur of momentary feeling and without regard to yesterday and tomorrow. His reflexes are generous but his foolishness about Rosamond's nature, and about women generally, stems from a carelessness that he does nothing to hinder. It is the same with his professional life when it comes to the petty politics of Middlemarch. When a particular vote must be taken on a particular issue, Lydgate finds the complexity of the issue annoying. Whichever way he began to incline, "there was something to make him wince; and being a proud man, he was a little exasperated at being obliged to wince." His solution is to avoid choice. "However it was, he did not distinctly say to himself on which side he would vote" and devoted himself to resentment at being forced by what is not even directly a medical issue. His ruminations make him late to the meeting, where his vote is most conspicuous in breaking a tie, and his actual action is the foolish reflex of the moment which has in it none of the generosity or clarity he can muster alone in his chambers (ch. 18).

The portrayal of the Lydgates' marriage is justly celebrated. It is a masterpiece of misconception on the part of the two participants. Rosamond's mind is not large enough for luxuries to look small in, so she cannot possibly understand the life of professional dedication her husband has in mind; and it has never occurred to Lydgate that his wife could oppose his will in anything, much less oppose it successfully. "Poor Lydgate!" exclaims the narrator, "or shall I say, Poor Rosamond! Each lived in a world of which the other knew nothing" (p. 123; ch. 16). When they rapidly become financially embarrassed by careless spending on furniture and china, Lydgate attempts to order his affairs by economies and comes up against his wife's terrifying unsusceptibility to influence. When he gives orders, Rosamond calmly countermands them, going behind his back time and again with a serene confidence that she understands things better, and that things should be ordered as she likes. He begins to think of Rosamond in the same breath with Madame Laure, his first love, who had the same calm way of violating his most basic assumptions about what would or could be reasonable. The contrast between Rosamond and Dorothea is one that occurs even to Lydgate and it is everywhere obvious in the novel. Compared to Dorothea, Rosamond is unsusceptible to influence, she will not learn what things cost, and has no power of sympathy. Dorothea is "open, ardent, and not in the least self-admiring," though her remarks to others are occasionally "not without a scorching quality. If Miss Brooke ever attained perfect meekness, it would not be for lack of inward fire" (pp. 9–10; ch. 1). Rosamond, on the other hand, is conscious of little but her own blameless perfections. "Though she would never do anything that was disagreeable to her," she was industrious and occupied most of all "in being from morning till night her own standard of a perfect lady, having always an audience in her own consciousness" (p. 124; ch. 16); (no mental conflict here); she "was not a fiery young lady and had no sharp answers, but she meant to live as she pleased" (p. 219; ch. 31). Lydgate thinks of these contrasts at one crisis, one in which he recognizes the hopelessness of a common understanding with his wife.

Rosamond's response to his urgent insistence that they must alter their spending contrasts in every way to Dorothea's response, made in similar words, to the news of her husband's illness. Rosamond's emphasis is everything, when she faces the bottomless financial difficulties that she has shared in making and that Lydgate requires her help in resolving. " 'What can *I* do, Tertius?' said Rosamond, turning her eyes on him. . . . Rosamond's thin utterance threw into the words, 'What can *I* do!' as much neutrality as they could hold. He did not storm in indignation—he felt too sad a sinking of the heart" (p. 434; ch. 58). Rosamond's silvery neutrality contrasts in Lydgate's mind jarringly with the urgent appeal from Dorothea when he has told her the full extent of Casaubon's illness. " 'Tell me what I can do. . . . Oh, you are a wise man, are you not? You know all about life and death. Advise me. Think what I can do.' . . . For years after Lydgate remembered the impression produced in him by this involuntary appeal—this cry from soul to soul. . ." (p. 214; ch. 30). And it tells with some irony that when he first met Dorothea he concluded that she was not his "style of woman." It is Miss Vincy, on the contrary, who looks at things "from the proper feminine angle" and "is what a woman ought to be" (pp. 69–70; ch. 11). When he fully learns the limits of his wife's window-less mind, he faces the most important choice of his life, but it is not a choice conveniently presented on account all at once. Resolve can be wrought up for emergencies more easily than maintained during days and weeks of tiny pressures.

Two things are necessary for Lydgate, once he has recognized that his wife is not the relief from care that he expected; he must get out of debt and he must subdue Rosamond's will to his more encompassing vision of possibilities. His professional success as a scientist, something he cherishes with the most selfless and generous resolve, depends upon it. But his resolve on these matters is not firm enough, or persistent enough soon enough. His response to an offer of help from Mr. Farebrother, trifling as it may seem, tells an important story. While Lydgate can admit his financial need to himself, he cannot face mentioning it to others, however sympathetic they may be. Mr. Farebrother is his friend, and a wise man, and also a man for whom Lydgate has done a service. But Lydgate freezes at Farebrother's offer of help with his pressing financial problems. "The suggestion that the Vicar discerned his need of a service in return made him shrink into unconquerable reticence. Besides, behind all making of such offers what else must come?—that he should 'mention his case,' imply that he wanted specific things. At that moment, suicide seemed easier" (p. 472; ch. 63). Such a confession of need, for one as concerned as Lydgate about keeping above the world, seems like a form of suicide because it would obscure that inner sense of distinction that he carries around with him; it comes even ahead of his professional ambition and it depends on such reticence. This motive, the commonness of not wanting to be common, is linked in every way with his defeat by Rosamond. He cannot see his way clear of hindrances in time to resist strongly against her pinching narrowness. His failure in the end is a failure of energy. "Perhaps if he had been strong enough to persist in his determination to be the more because she was the less, that evening might have had a better issue. If his energy could have borne down that check, he might still have wrought on Rosamond's vision and will. . . . But poor Lydgate had a throbbing pain within him, and his energy had fallen short of its task" (p. 556; ch. 75).

The "central unacted possibility" in *Middlemarch* is marriage between Lydgate and Dorothea.[4] His vocation as a healer would satisfy Dorothea's need for service, and her generous understanding would support Lydgate's highest ambition. But they meet fewer than half a dozen times in the novel. At her engagement dinner he scarcely notices her, except to conclude she is not his "sort of woman." They meet twice about medical business when Casaubon is ill, and once about hospital affairs. When they finally meet about purely personal problems, the mistaken gossip about his role in Raffles's death and the financial embarrassment of being indebted to Bulstrode, their lives have taken definite courses that do not include intimacy between the two of them. They remain relative strangers, influencing each other's lives at a distance.

Daniel Deronda

Such a relationship is central in the last novel, *Daniel Deronda* (1876), but here George Eliot conceives a kind of intimacy, possible between relative strangers and yet not the intimacy of marriage. Gwendolen Harleth and Daniel Deronda also meet fewer than half a dozen times in the novel: once by chance in a Continental gambling casino, once just before her marriage and once just after, and once by chance in an Italian hotel. The link between Gwendolen and Deronda is not marriage, though the possibility occurs to both of them, and not easy friendship or neighborly contact; it is rather the intimacy of confession. Gwendolen makes of Deronda a sort of "external con-science" in helping her avoid self-destructiveness, a result by now so familiar in George Eliot's novels in those characters who cannot recon-cile their ideas and their actions. Confession, of the sort Lydgate and Bulstrode and Casaubon avoided, is the reunion of idea and act. Gwendolen accomplishes this reunion through her odd relationship with Daniel Deronda, in a novel that brings together a variety of na-tional and racial and personal opposites. The confessional relationship at the center, an intimacy not leading to marriage, sets the tone for a novel that goes farther than ever toward the mythic structures of experience uniting even the most diverse material. We have in this novel both the brilliant representation of manners characteristic of earlier works and the strange but equally brilliant representation of the psychic life that lies behind manners, as behind all ritual, giving them their depth and resonance.

Daniel Deronda is an English novel that begins and ends abroad. It opens at a roulette table in a Continental gambling casino and at a point of intersection between the two main plots. Gwendolen Harleth is winning at this table, until she draws the passing, but not indiffer-ent, attention of a stranger. This first encounter with Daniel De-ronda, and her swift sense that he looks at her with disapproval, casts an "evil eye" on her winning streak. It is the first in the series of encounters between them that knits together the deeply divided world in this novel. Of the eight books, the first three make two sep-arate intersecting loops backward in time, each tracing the history of

one of the central pair before the moment their paths cross in Leubronn. The subsequent five books follow the parallel lives of Gwendolen and Deronda, alternating between one and the other and
gradually shifting in focus from her story to his.

The first three books interest us mainly in Gwendolen's character,
and a delightful character it is. "The Spoiled Child" (book 1) deals
with the heroine, a young lady who means to marry well and to do as
she likes. The book ends with her introduction to her future husband,
Henleigh Grandcourt, a bachelor so eligible from a material stand-
point that the neighbors, the Arrowpoints, are thinking of him for
their daughter before he has set foot in the neighborhood.[5] "The
Meeting Streams" (book 2) finds Gwendolen in flight from Grandcourt, frightened by his cold manners and by the revelation of his secret past. By the time he pursues her to Leubronn she has just left
again, summoned home unexpectedly by the family's financial failure;
Grandcourt instead encounters his distant relative Daniel Deronda,
and in midbook the narrative shifts to his story and loops backward
over his past, bringing him to the point where he meets his future
wife, Mirah Lapidoth, a Jewess and an alien in England, as she is on
the brink of committing suicide. "Maiden's Choosing" (book 3) shifts
from Mirah, lodged with Deronda's friends the Meyricks in London,
to Gwendolen, who now chooses to marry Grandcourt hoping to save
herself from relative financial hardship, and finally to Catherine
Arrowpoint, who chooses to follow her heart and to marry Herr
Klesmer the musician, even though he is wholly objectionable to her
family on the grounds that he is a Jew for whom she probably will
forfeit her fortune. The parallels in book 1 thus contrast Gwendolen,
on the brink of a momentous choice, with two other women in similar positions, one ready to drown herself in despair and the other prepared to give up her wealth to follow her own course. Mirah's
decision to give up, hindered at the last minute by Deronda, and
Catherine's decision to fight, suggest alternative courses of action to
the conventional one into which Gwendolen drifts.

Gwendolen's story is a tale of developing secret life, and the monu-
mental effort, even the life and death struggle required for her to escape it. From the outset Gwendolen is charming, beautiful, and
quick-witted. She means to do as she likes but, unlike Rosamond
Vincy, she is very susceptible to influence. Her instinctive aversion
to Grandcourt, like her fears of solitude or her hopelessness about her
inability to love people, are redeeming signs of a responsive nature;

she has a sense of her limits that is the basis for growth. She is untrained for any serious occupation and means to marry well so as to avoid (as the blunt Klesmer has occasion to tell her), the need to do, or know, or understand anything exactly (p. 297; ch. 23). Despite Grandcourt's money, her personal dislike for him is such that, when she discovers the existence of his mistress Lydia Glasher and their two children, she feels relief at being freed from the necessity of choosing. Even when Grandcourt renews his suit, and she is considerably more in need of money, she is still repelled by him at the same time as she is drawn to his wealth. Reversing her decision not to see him, she is without clear direction when the final choice offers itself. "She seemed to herself to be, after all, only drifted towards the tremendous decision:—but drifting depends upon something besides the currents, when the sails have been set beforehand" and Gwendolen drifts into an engagement (p. 348; ch. 27). She has broken her promise to Lydia Glasher that she will not marry Grandcourt, and she knows the full baseness of her motives. She expects to keep all this a secret, and forget the problematic Mrs. Glasher, but she does not yet know the full baseness of her husband's motives. He knows her secret and marries her out of a perverse delight in mastery. With Gwendolen's acceptance of his terms Grandcourt begins his empire of fear.

Daniel Deronda's brief history is that of someone with very little history to tell. Raised as the nephew of Sir Hugo Mallinger, Deronda's first painful awareness of being "different" comes at the age of thirteen when he learns from his tutor that wealthy men sometimes raise their illegitimate sons as "nephews." Sir Hugo merely assures him that he lost both his parents when he was quite young, but Deronda nourishes a deep-seated uncertainty about his identity. This uncertainity encourages in him a sympathy for people who are confused or struggling, and prevents him from seeking a place in a society where his birth might be always a matter of question or even disgrace. Though Sir Hugo intends him "to have the education of an English gentleman," Deronda's school friends' talk of home and parents aggravates and mortifies his sense of "entailed disadvantage." His sympathy is generous but born of irresolution. At Cambridge "he might have taken a high place if his motives had been of a more pushing sort, and if he had not, instead of regarding studies as instruments of success, hampered himself with the notion that they were to feed motive and opinion—a notion which set him criticising methods and arguing against his freight and harness when he should have been using all his might to pull." He inclines to no particular track, and longs for "that sort of apprenticeship to life which would not shape him too definitely." Such "reflective hesitation" becomes merely an "excuse for lingering longer than others in a state of social neutrality" (pp. 218–20; ch. 16). His habit of drifting in a boat on the Thames, evidently a corollary of his mental habits, suddenly gives him an interest when he discovers Mirah Lapidoth attempting to drown herself.

The remaining five books alternate between Gwendolen and Deronda, although the book titles refer increasingly to his story and less to hers, as his wider horizons encompass her narrower ones. In book 4 "Gwendolen Gets Her Choice," and pays the price for it. At the time of her engagement "her 'Yes' entailed so little." But her marriage soon entails a harsh awakening from her aimless pursuit of self-interest. To complement her own will, which "had seemed imperious in its small girlish sway . . . she had found a will like that of a crab or a boa-constrictor which goes on pinching or crushing without alarm at thunder." A few months of marriage seems "half her life" and after every new shock of humiliation from Grandcourt, "she tried to adjust herself and seize her old supports—proud concealment, trust in new excitements" (pp. 477–78; ch. 35). But book 4 includes another history, quite apart from Gwendolen's "Choice" as Daniel Deronda searches for Mirah's brother through the pawnshops and bookstores of London. His efforts to help Mirah find her lost brother and mother lead him into a world of Jewish life quite separate within English society and into contact with a kind of vision wholly unlike that of his familiar society. Mordecai Cohen, the chief spokesman for this vision, is Mirah's brother and a Zionist seeking a successor to carry on his work once he dies from the consumption already well-advanced upon him.

"Mordecai" (book 5) begins with the first of Gwendolen's confessions to Deronda (these are discussed below). Mordecai's insistence that Deronda be his successor understandably causes that fastidious young gentleman some difficulty. He finds Mordecai's ideal vision of an international community of nations a congenial vision and one devoid of the partisanship that he himself instinctively dislikes. But, as this novel makes so clear, ideals seem to be one thing, and actuality quite another. "Enthusiasm, we know, dwells at ease among ideas, tolerates garlic breathed in the middle ages, and sees no shabbiness in the official trappings of classic processions: it gets squeamish when ideals press upon it as something warmly incarnate, and can hardly face them without fainting." The fervour of such enthusiasm "is feeble compared with the enthusiasm that keeps unslacked and where there is no danger, no challenge—nothing but impartial mid-day falling on common-place, perhaps half-repulsive, objects which are really the beloved ideas made flesh. Here undoubtedly lies the chief poetic energy:—in the force of imagination that pierces or exalts the solid fact, instead of floating among cloud pictures" (pp. 430–31; ch. 33). This passage—with its echoes of the similar passage in *Adam Bede* (chapter 17), and of the passage in *Middlemarch* (chapter 22) where Ladislaw says Dorothea is a poem—is filled with George Eliot's emphasis on incarnations; and it is clearly critical of Deronda's squeamishness. Still, Mordecai's claim on Deronda is strange, bordering on the bizarre, and Deronda's shrinking seems thoroughly understandable. One of the difficult tasks George Eliot sets for herself in this novel is the task of moving Deronda, and her readers, from his understandable disbelief and reluctance, gradually, to belief and acceptance of Mordecai's charge; and making it seem even reasonable.

"Revelations" (book 6) includes not only more of Gwendolen's confessions to Deronda but also the revelation that Mordecai is Mirah's long-sought brother, and the revelation by Sir Hugo that Deronda's mother, whom he thought long-dead, is alive and wishes to see him. "Mother and Son" (book 7) takes Deronda to Genoa for the two extraordinary visits with his mother, now called the Princess Halm-Eberstein since her marriage to a Russian nobleman, but once the great singer Alcharisi who sacrificed knowingly even her son for the sake of a brilliant career as an artist. Even the fulfillment of a goal so congenial to George Eliot's vision of human possibilities has its heavy price, and Alcharisi pays hers when she faces death and is brought by the burden of fatal illness to confess the secret she spent a lifetime guarding. In confessing to her son she gives in at last to the imperative father whose orthodox Judaism allowed no room for her life. The parallels with Mirah, a singer with a voice that is exquisite but too small for the stage, and Gwendolen, who idly imagines taking her indifferently trained voice on stage in preference to marrying Grandcourt, are just part of the richness in this magnificent portrait.

The relation of mother and son, and the revelation of Deronda's Jewish ancestry, while intensive enough for him, also has influence in store for Gwendolen, though she is yet unaware of it. Grandcourt has taken her to Genoa against her will, on a boating excursion, tightening his already pinching grasp upon her resistant will. The boating

accident in which Grandcourt drowns releases Gwendolen from him
but plunges her into a state of grief that is the opposite of sorrow for
his loss. She has wished for his death. She has watched him die. And
she has not saved him. The accumulated guilt she feels consequent on
her marriage threatens to overwhelm her, and Deronda's presence on
his own momentous errand brings them together most intensely just
at the moment he begins to make particular plans for his life in quite
another direction. Gwendolen returns to England in book 8, "Fruit
and Seed," expecting to continue relying on him, but he returns to
England to marry Mirah, and to accept the vocation that Mordecai
has offered. In her reliance on him, on his visits, Gwendolen "no
more thought of the Lapidoth's—the little jewess and her brother—
as likely to make a difference in her destiny, than of the fermenting
political and social leaven which was making a difference in the history of the world" (pp. 842–43; ch. 65). She is still thinking of her
life in relation to his, when he tells her that he is a Jew and intends
to go to Palestine to work for the cause of Zionism. This news enters
like an earthquake into her life, and she is for the "first time dis-
lodged from her supremacy in her own world, and getting a sense
that her horizon was but a dipping onward of an existence with which
her own was revolving" (p. 876; ch. 69). In giving up her interested
claim on Deronda, she undertakes a "difficult rectitude" toward him
that is a heavy burden, but she bears it, for once, with success.

The crux of the novel is the relation between the two central plots,
which are kept separate with great deliberateness and which touch one
another with communications between Gwendolen and Deronda that
are not ordinary moments. The personal differences between Gwendolen and Deronda are obvious enough. She is a woman, he is a man;
she has no money, he has as much as he wants; her education is indifferent, his is the best available; her ambition is concentrated in personal supremacy, his is deflected among infinite possibilities. He has
everything materially, and yet he cannot assert himself; she feels the
pressure of material wants, and habitually asserts herself to satisfy
them. But there are deep similarities between them that confirm the
universality of those shared structures hinted at in so many ways in
this novel. For very different reasons they both have difficulty taking
their place in society, that is, a difficulty with vocation. Both make
the inefficient use of their energies that encourages a kind of passivity
and threatens will. She gambles in search of passion, Deronda wants
to be called or chosen. Both drift to avoid choice. Both muster cre-

ative self-assertion when they discover a purpose beyond personal success. Their entire relation to one another embodies that "separateness
with communication" that is Deronda's motto for his position in relation to the ideas he inherits from his grandfather (p. 792; ch. 60).
Separateness is the basis for form, unity. It is the trust of another,
different as Feuerbach says and yet alike, that makes the power of
confession, and this power unifies the separate plots through Gwendolen's confessions to Deronda.

   The power of confession lies in trust, if not of oneself then of another. The inner reunion of thought and action depends largely on
the presence of an outer voice of conscience. "It is hard to say how
much we could forgive ourselves if we were secure from judgment by
another. . . . In this way our brother may be in the stead of God to
us, and his opinion which has pierced even to the joints and marrow
may be our virtue in the making" (pp. 832–33; ch. 64). As Gwendolen's habits of proud concealment fail her in her deepening unhappiness, she begins to rely on talks with Deronda. In confessing her
feelings to him she finds a "deep rest" from the self-suppression that
is numbing her personality (p. 405, ch. 31; p. 464, ch. 35). She has
married a man with a withered heart, though she was warned, and
for reasons she will not admit, and so she must carry on and on, her
mouth all smiling pretense and her heart and mind all despair. She
pretends that her life is the brilliant thing she wanted it to be, hiding
the reality behind a paralyzed mask of satisfaction. Her family and
friends are well-meaning, materialistic, will-less, and cannot be
trusted with her secret. Her uncle Gascoigne has a comfortable sense
that Gwendolen is worth spending a little money on because she will
bring in a good marriage offer, a sense of the transactional value of
her life that has an almost grotesque vulgarity despite his congenial
easy-going nature. Her mamma, Mrs. Davilow, has never exerted authority over Gwendolen, but instead submits to her. Consequently
Gwendolen's hold on Deronda is her hold on sanity, and he feels the
intensity of her grasp. "She was bent on confession" and he dreaded
it. "He was not a priest" (p. 754; ch. 56). But after her husband's
drowning he supports her through her deepest despair. "And if I had
told you, and knew it was in your mind," she confides, "it would
have less power over me. I hoped and trusted in that" (p. 758; ch.
56). Even though, as Deronda ascertains, she probably could not have
saved Grandcourt, *she* knows that when he cried out and sank for the
last time, she withheld her hand, and her "heart said, 'Die!' " (761).

Gwendolen is much in need of the "outer conscience" (p. 833; ch. 64) she finds in Deronda or, more exactly, in her idea of Deronda, and it is something she clings to in the absence of other guides as to a life raft in a storm. The final step for Gwendolen is acceptance of facts as they actually are, especially and beginning with those concerning Deronda. With her acceptance that things are not as she wishes them to be, she gives up the secret life that plagued her. Her self-assertion subsides "before the bewildering vision of [Deronda's] wide-ranging purposes in which she felt herself reduced to a mere speck." From the full sense of her supremacy Gwendolen has traveled mountainous distances to reach this new sense of a vast world that knows nothing of her claims. Such resignation is the first time she has accepted her separateness and freedom, and her responsibility for her own course. Gwendolen's acknowledgment to Deronda of the separateness of their lives is the essential starting point for any union between them; and that acknowledgment depends on the reunion in her own life between thought and action.

The reunion of ideas and actuality accomplished by confession is a subject with much broader significance in *Daniel Deronda* than its meaning for a single woman. There are deep divisions represented in the novel that are not solved by the few individual confessions and that leave behind questions rather than resolutions. A chief problem is the apparent lack of psychological realism in the Deronda plot, especially in comparison with the Gwendolen plot, and this problem has been the subject of much critical discussion.[6] The Deronda plot seems too full of allegorical significances. His Jewishness is prefigured in ways that are considered arbitrary; he looks like a choirboy, he is called "Ishmael," Mordecai claims him as if he were a Jew, Mirah will only marry a Jew, and then, miraculously, he turns out to be a Jew. There is, in short, too much Idea present, suggesting that the Deronda plot is part of a teaching project on George Eliot's part and reflective of a loss of authorial control for the sake of special pleading.

This approach is misconceived. It is true that George Eliot sought to give a portrait of Jewish life that was positive: something unusual in English literary tradition. And it is true that Deronda's woodenness, which can be explained as a symptom of his preference for a disembodied mental existence, and as a criticism of his limitations, does compare unfavorably in psychological realism with the scenes in which Gwendolen flourishes (the premier value of psychological realism remains an open question). And it is true that the author's language in the Deronda plot is full of visionary vocabulary and religious value quite absent from the other plot. But careful reading shows that there is considerably more to it than that, as one might suspect from knowing George Eliot's mastery of her craft. Whatever this division is for, it clearly is not an accident.

In understanding the relation between the two plots we recognize, first of all, that there is allegorical significance in the Gwendolen plot, too, though it is less obvious for many reasons. Grandcourt's name, his reptilian nature, the poisoned jewels that bring the "furies" across his threshold, the name "Harleth," all belong to a bourgeois world of material things that has significance to its adherents of an ultimate kind, one comparable for them to the meaning that Zionism and Judaism have for the other plot. Conversely, we recognize that the Deronda plot has many sustained and significant realistic effects, including the sense of place associated with the Cohens, Mordecai's room and the group of artisan friends that calls itself the Philosophers Club; the streets of London and the anonymous life of the city come through especially clearly in this plot, and fittingly so since it is a world ignored by the privileged caste.

These different values in plot and style correspond to a deep division in the novel between the world of ideas and the world of things, a division that is quite intentional on George Eliot's part. The mistake of Western philosophy since Parmenides, she wrote in an essay, is the separation of ideas from things.[7] The dualism informs the social analysis in both plots. The English gentry care about things: property, and passing it on. The Arrowpoints' first response to their Catherine's declaration in favor of Herr Klesmer is to consider immediately what candidates might be available to inherit her fortune and thus keep it among the "right" people. Despite its trappings, this is the same vulgarity of exclusiveness evident in the humbler Dodsons and Tullivers. Gwendolen's uncle spends money on her as bait for a rich husband. It is little wonder that she is mercenary; it is a form of class devotion. Despite Mrs. Arrowpoint's dabbling in classics, the people who care most about ideas in the novel are Jews (though not all Jews); they care about ideas and about embodying them in art or in political forms, partly because, like Mordecai, they are not absorbed in the material universe governed by the bankrupt English aristocracy.

The novel deliberately poses the problem of reconciliation between the two plots and two modes, and the problem touches directly on the predispositions of readers. The ambitious joining of English and Jewish plots and prototypes can make the Jewish part seem foreign but, as one critic pertinently asks, "Foreign to whom? The 'English' part of the novel is impervious to such alienation and is approved by Anglo-Saxon readers of whatever critical persuasion. The 'Jewish' part was lauded by Jewish scholars and Eliot was gratified by the approbation." To readers familiar with the Zionist movement and with Palestine, Deronda's emigration would appear realistic; to those not so familiar, "Deronda is seen not as going to another place on earth but as taking straight off for the clouds."[8] The novel seems to suggest that George Eliot was quite aware how, for an Englishman like Deronda, educated in all the best schools and fastidious in his tastes, going off to Palestine to pursue a career as a nonpartisan Zionist would have in it shocks that could compare with those visited upon Gwendolen. In any case, it is important to see that the novel does not pose the sides of this dualism as alternatives; it poses the choice as a mistake to remedy, as all things are remedied, in the slow interaction of individuals and institutions, and beginning, indeed, with Gwendolen's accomplishment in confession. It is not ideas or things but ideas and things, even ideas *as* things, that is the motivating conception in this work. The incarnate world is the only one for human consideration.

The differences in language between the two plots are important because to George Eliot a conception is inseparable from its expression or incarnate presentation. In all her work it is clear how differences in consciousness and experience can act like differences of native language, making the communications essential to culture difficult to sustain. All such systems of apprehension are definitive in their influence, but also partial. In this novel she actually dramatizes the differences between such systems. The language and hence the conceptualizatons that English readers take to be "natural" are shown to be only one way of conceiving things. It would not suit George Eliot's purpose in *Daniel Deronda* for the Deronda plot to be more like the Gwendolen plot; each plot has something the other does not, both of value and of limitation, so the matter of choice, some search for finality, is not allowed as a serious possibility.

The obvious example of such deliberate effects is the artificiality and mannerism of Mordecai's speech. His intensity contrasts explicitly with the drawling manners of "that antipole of all enthusiasm called 'a man of the world' " (p. 552; ch. 40): Grandcourt for example, but also Gascoigne and good Sir Hugo. When Mordecai takes leave of Deronda on one occasion, asking when he will return, he says in effect that he wants to know before he dies that Deronda will continue his work and that, even though Deronda has not accepted, he still feels encouraged that one day he will. Grandcourt or Sir Hugo would likely have put such thoughts, if they could have had them, into elliptical, drawling speech—showing a careless air of mastery, and even a trivializing of particular details. Mordecai, however, talks completely differently. He speaks like a prophet. "The days I wait now are longer than the years of my strength. Life shrinks: what was but a tithe is now the half. My hope abides in you. . . . This is come to pass, and the rest will come" (p. 564; ch. 40). At the very least this captures a difference in mental poise between this man and people like Mr. Vandernoodt and Grandcourt. Mordecai talks differently because he thinks and acts differently. He would no more refer to Gwendolen as a "fine gal" than he would change his vocation.

The thought that ideas and enactments are one, has a special place in George Eliot's conception of the social and human world. When Gwendolen awkwardly refers to Deronda's concern for "ideas, knowledge, wisdom, and all that," he replies that all objects of interest and affection are "a mixture—half persons and half ideas" (pp. 470–71; ch. 35). This is something the Jews and artists in the novel seem to understand more consciously than the English aristocrats. Mirah says that whatever people call beautiful and best must also be true because "it is always there," like a myth that "lives as an idea." Even something exotic and strange, Deronda adds, like a Buddhist legend, "is like a passionate word . . . the exaggeration is a flash of fervour. It is an extreme image of what is happening every day" (p. 523; ch. 37). "All actions men put a little thought into are ideas" (p. 583; ch. 42), says one of Mordecai's friends at the Philosophers Club; and the group, whose trades are lens-grinding, wood-inlaying, shoemaking, watchmaking, and bookselling, embodies the conception. Such unity is the goal of Mordecai's Zionism, as well as his final prayer. He proposes to light the torch of visible community, like the settlers of North America: "what had they to form a polity with but memories of Europe corrected by the vision of a better?" In the same way, a new Judea, "poised between East and West" will be a "covenant of reconciliation" (p. 597; ch. 42). The Shemah, a Hebrew prayer that Mordecai utters on his deathbed, is a "confession of divine Unity" and a fitting final echo for a novel with so deep and consistent an emphasis on the reunion between thought and action.

Chapter Six
Conclusion

George Eliot is the novelist of freedom. Her work shows, with an irony she fully appreciated, that freedom is a human necessity, that is, an inescapable condition of experience. Many of her characters seek escape from the pressures of their circumstances through belief in some nonhuman source of order that might temporarily ease or even numb their sense of the "hard unaccommodating Actual." Many of her plots are motivated by versions of this flight from conditions, either to alcohol and other "opiates," or to abstractions like "right" or "truth." What alcohol and abstractions have in common in these cases is the function of relief: shifting from human beings the sense of their individual responsibility and with it their individual opportunity. Responsibility and opportunity are one in George Eliot's world. In a spirit similar to Feuerbach's she encourages studious attention to the actual, particular conditions of endeavor because it is there alone that achievement is fostered, and there alone that hope can be disappointed or satisfied.

In her move away from transcendental metaphysics of any kind George Eliot focuses attention on the inseparability of ideas and things. An idea is not something aloof from feeling, any more than intention is aloof from act. In demonstrating the confirmatory power of habit—the fact that one is what one does and repeats—she shows how incarnate "ideas" always are. These repetitive acts *are* the "ideas" of one's life, and not those flattering self-reflections that can be shaped in conscious deliberation quite apart from activity. The reliable guides to life are immanent, tangible things; and in turn, tangible things in the human world all embody ideas and intentions. In the human situation as George Eliot presents it idea and act are one. Her novels show how the conditions of freedom make it easy to dissociate idea and act, and how this dissociation usually brings self-betrayal and ruin. Her novels also show those powers that unify idea and act and that foster the self-conscious exercise of inevitable freedom.

A George Eliot novel always demonstrates the creative power of free acts, whether those acts initiate new departures or suppress them and whether the result is productive or destructive. Because idea and act are one, the humble gesture can be much more forceful than the more dramatic ones precisely because they elude direct notice and hence elude control. The world-historical individuals, or the celebrities, or the "geniuses" are not the main movers of history in George Eliot's works, and probably not even real creatures so much as a way of naturalizing discontents. After all, if a person who accomplishes something is fundamentally extraordinary, then ordinary persons need not feel called to emulate them. The commitment to humble life evident in her works stems not from half-evaporated Christian views but from her knowledge of the power that inheres in domestic arrangements where the habits of centuries receive incremental reinforcement or restraint. The activity of all individuals past and present—a sum that is always changing its definition—constitutes the particular circumstance of every individual freedom; this invisible yet all-important creation is what George Eliot's novels reveal and dramatize. It is easy enough to see a crime and to calculate a punishment—to concentrate, in short, on the exchange of offenses; George Eliot's work is directed to the more difficult and more sustaining recognition of the creative influences that surround and support us, and that we use and profit from without even fully recognizing them.

The artificiality of culture—its independence from the calm determinism of nature—is always evident in the novels; George Eliot emphasizes the artificiality of culture because it is what makes possible our profound freedoms. Because culture has been made by human beings it can be changed by them; it does not belong to one configuration in the eternal fitness of things but rather to a historical moment. Ordinary beings function just as artists do, in that they have both material to work with and a vision to follow. To succeed, ordinary beings, like artists, must base their projects on the actual possibilities of their material rather than on some fantasy of hope unsustained by reason, either internal or "external" reason. Just as an artist is doomed who tries to make a sculpture out of paint, so characters in her novels are doomed who use their imagination to avoid circumstantial facts rather than to pierce and subdue them. Such unsuccessful people tend to hold inflexible views, to believe in their own rectitude, and, consequently, to be passive. On the other hand, the artist, like the ordinary being, has full commitment to provisional views, recognizes the limits of all authority including his or her own, and hence can be active. Happiness and grief come to all alike but only the creative person can exert some control over the process. The sense George Eliot's novels give that every act has consequences demonstrates the power of choice and, far from showing individual helplessness, shows that it matters what we do.

Culture in George Eliot's work is not only artificial, it is also collective. Nobody owns it; everybody supports it, and everybody includes not only the inhabitants of a particular historical moment but also those long dead. It is for her a constant source of wonder that an individual's acts live on in others "even when they have quite gone away from the mind in which they were born" (Letters, 4:158). One finds in her fiction a vision of culture as conservation, culture as a reserve of order and possibility as well as of limitation. The idea that nothing is lost, as she wrote to a friend, "is one of my favorite altars where I oftenest go to contemplate and to seek for invigorating motive" (Letters, 3:316). If everyone has a source of belief and emphasis,—an "altar"—this is George Eliot's: the idea that nothing is lost. Only someone who does not understand George Eliot could find disheartening the passage at the end of Middlemarch describing the "diffusive influence" of Dorothea: "the growing good of the world is partly dependent on unhistoric acts; and that things are not so ill with you and me as they might have been, is half owing to the number who lived faithfully a hidden life, and rest in unvisited tombs." It is the anonymous lives of a multitude of unique, ordinary individuals, that has made possible our civilities. To find the anonymity of the effort depressing implies a taste for World-Historical Action, or for Remarkable Genius, that George Eliot sees as another form of special pleading to justify inactivity or shabby achievement. One's influence lives, not apart from or above, but within and through the particular conditions of collective life, and in its traditions, its languages, its accumulated power of consciousness. The power to make instruments of those conditions requires a power of trust in others, because in other people conditions are most alive and most immediately available.

George Eliot's view of culture, as expressed in her novels and essays, differs significantly from the more famous and still influential one of Matthew Arnold; the elevation of his view to a Victorian norm and the confusion of her idea of culture with Arnold's may have contributed to the extensive misreading of George Eliot's cultural vision. Hers involves the constant action of individual talent on tradition, changing and altering its entire homeostatic balance at every moment. Like Arnold she does see culture as the highest mental result of human endeavor, and like him she regards partisanship and factionalism as "a chief curse of our time, a chief obstacle to true culture" (*Letters*, 6:418). But unlike Arnold, whose disinterestedness suggests removal, she stresses unavoidable participation. Her culture is incomplete, ever-changing, open-ended, incarnate in its participants and their works; her novels engage her readers; it may be in the oxygen of a country village or in the gas-poisoned atmosphere of a casino, but it is never in the ozone of Arnold's "tradition."[1]

The very principle of individual diversity in culture that evolves from the fact of human freedom creates a complexity in which conflict is inevitable. An artificial, aggregate, collective venture without any secret principle of unity, culture requires that individuals be capable of sustaining conflict. The conflict of valid claims, explained in her Antigone essay and demonstrated in all her novels, can interfere with creativity (for example in *The Mill on the Floss*), but there is no escape from conflict given the conditions of human experience. Creative power is the power to deal with conflict either within an individual or between individuals. Mordecai's "resistant" energy is preferable to Deronda's flaccid passivity; Ladislaw's power to cross the expectations of others is part of his independence; Maggie's conflict with her family is ultimately destructive but it is also the best thing about her. It is crucial to see that for George Eliot conflict does not necessarily mean social breakdown, nor does it mean that the dual roles of self-determination and social duty are incompatible. Conflict is inevitable to growing life, as it breaks through limits and repudiates finality. George Eliot presents no plan for unifying all valid claims or for abolishing conflict, but instead she offers the zig-zag interest of perpetual action and reaction between individuals and institutions, mending both little by little, which is "the only way in which human things can be mended" (*Essays*, 205).

Like her master, Walter Scott, George Eliot did not believe in first causes, or ultimate ends, or single explanations of history; and her outlook is more complicated and radical than the one usually attributed to her. The workings of the human universe are a mixed entangled affair, overseen by no single mind and united only by the broad facts of life and death. No single mind can grasp more than a few patterns, or realize more than a few possibilities, or concentrate on more than one corner of the vast range of relevancies. All an individual's interest and attention, in vocation as in art, should be fixed not on endings or goals but on experiments in life: on ways of discovering what he or she is capable of, and on giving particular embodiment to one possibility at a time. George Eliot did not change her fundamental ideas during her artist's career; her mind was well matured by the time she began writing fiction. But an obvious aesthetic development in her work does exist, and it suggests a more profound development than just that of a writer's style. The changes in style and subject from *Adam Bede* to *Daniel Deronda* do reflect, as U. C. Knoepflmacher has observed, a classical development from eclogue to epic,[2] a movement that was probably not unconscious on George Eliot's part. But beyond this, the changes reflect the development of an entire culture. Treatment of the rural, even feudal society of the early novels gives way to a portrait of Renaissance politics, and eventually arrives in the later novels at the modern society of nineteenth-century England, in the last novel even anticipating twentieth-century focus on Israel and on the political and cultural problems inspired by Middle-East conflict. The detachment from traditional authority thus finds full representation in George Eliot's work, beginning with the testing of feudal loyalty and with the strong "natural" sense of place in *Adam Bede*. *Romola*, on the other hand, begins with the soaring Angel of the Dawn looking at human particulars from tremendous distance in time and space, and *Felix Holt* opens with a famous meditation on mobility. The development of that detachment, so evident in the last novel, is important both to her subject in her fictions and also to her narrative strategy. A character like Adam Bede, who stays in one place and does what his father did before him, has a sense of identity that remains tied to custom in a manner that is impossible and undesirable once he learns, as Bob Jakin learns in *The Mill on the Floss*, to pack up his profession and move it from place to place. In her cinematic prologues to the middle novels George Eliot emphasizes a detachment and mobility that her narrators constantly embody. Such mobility necessitates a detachment from place unthinkable for the denizens of Hayslope, but unavoidable for citizens of the world.

Reputation

George Eliot's reputation with her contemporaries was very high, and their general level of aesthetic judgment was often also remarkably high. E. S. Dallas, for example, wrote in 1872 about her narrator with a sophistication that was unsurpassed for nearly a century (see Gordon S. Haight's critical collection). Her public was large and international in scope, and her critics respectful. The best account of her contemporary reception—its extent, its high moments with *Adam Bede* and *Middlemarch* and low moments with *Romola*, its peculiarly Victorian agendas concerning social and moral issues—all are admirably and succinctly recounted in David Carroll's introduction to his collection of the best and more representative contemporary criticism (see bibliography, Critical Collections).

After her death, George Eliot's reputation underwent a sea-change from which it did not recover for fifty years. With the exception of Virginia Woolf's mixed tribute in 1919 (see Gordon S. Haight's edition of criticism), much of the criticism of that period now looks arrogant, condescending, and unresponsive to the texts she actually wrote. This phenomenon cannot be entirely explained by John Cross's edition of her letters and journals, but his edition did have a significant distorting influence on public perception of the writer. Left bereaved after less than a year of marriage, humorless Cross began building altars to her memory and (one's teeth rattle to think of it) destroying parts of the record that he felt were inappropriate for public attention. His *Life* was the only access to the author available until 1955 when Gordon S. Haight began publishing his impeccable edition of her letters. Cross's effort got some reinforcement from George Eliot's last publication, a collection of essays called *Impressions of Theophrastus Such* (1879); written after Lewes's death and published just before her own, the book sold heavily, but the writing seems heavy by comparison with the lively early essays and probably contributed to the distorted image of the author as sad genius.

The condescension has been so energetic and persistent, however, and is so transparently sexist in some cases, that Cross cannot be held responsible for the malaise that passed over George Eliot criticism for so many years. The condescension usually appears in one of three forms: an assumption of inadvertence in her aesthetic effects, as if they were the spontaneous overflow of uncontrolled personal yearnings; an assumption that her ideas are essentially derivative, originating with Lewes, Comte, Spencer, Feuerbach, anywhere but herself; and an assumption that her forward-looking views conflict with vestiges of Christian feeling, thus causing her to be contradictory. These three themes—the Aesthetic Inadvertence theme, the Intellectually

Derivative theme, and the Warmed-Over Christianity theme—do not hold up well under examination, when such examination is supplied. Too often, however, they have merely been repeated like critical mantras. In various ways they suggest that George Eliot is a mere contradictory female, controlled by powers greater than her own. One wonders, for example, why critics like Robert Liddell (*The Novels of George Eliot*, 1977) bother to write at all about an author they lack the power to appreciate; yet one recalls that even Henry James, who benefited from George Eliot's hospitality and notice, who borrowed considerably from her work, and who ought to have known better, still assumed rather too easily an attitude of condescension in reviewing her work (for James's self-absorbed behavior with Lewes and George Eliot see Haight's *Biography*, 513–14, and 416–17).

This tradition of condescension, though it has receded in influence, has not entirely disappeared. Some recent examples will give its flavor. "Although George Eliot abandoned her Christian faith she retained an irrational belief in a divine purpose. . . . All her novels have major flaws because she was afraid to face the realities of a world without God." This presents an author who acts inadvertently, succumbing to feeling that seems to be associated by this critic with fear. Another example of condescension is from a recent feminist article claiming that George Eliot was able to muster only "covert recognition of the truth she could not openly own." Another critic claims, of a particular view of nature, that it was one "George Eliot could not help affirming and attacking at the same time." An interpreter of *Romola* sees its modernity but feels compelled to assume this effect was mistaken because (it is taken for granted) George Eliot's religious "despair" forced her to recoil from her own strongest portraits and to lapse into "philosophic uncertainty." Her French biographer discusses her conflicting "optimism" and "pessimism" at some remove from the basis of her thought, despite his attention to her intellectual history. Such misconstructions have grown apace in George Eliot criticism and the way to avoid them is to begin with her writing and translation rather than with some extraneous system (whether "Victorian" or "Comtian" or "Hegelian") whose relevance for George Eliot has not been demonstrated. An allegedly Freudian interpretation of the novels, doing justice neither to Freud nor to George Eliot, claims for the fishing scene in *The Mill on the Floss*, "The setting is symbolic. The round pool is a perfect womb. . . . Maggie's one experience of unity with Tom seems to be linked with an unconscious memory of the womb, and we begin to see that Tom is, at one level, a mother substitute."[3]

Readers wishing to avoid these pitfalls are best advised to begin with George Eliot's novels and other writing, pursuing the general interests and issues that those suggest, and then to read criticism that does the same. Conventional wisdom about George Eliot, about the Victorians, or about the novel can rapidly lead her interpreter astray because she does not write from conventional bases. In separating moral and aesthetic issues, for example, we necessarily invoke a distinction and a habit of thought that her works deny. Even the most devoted readers will have felt that particular *frisson* of arriving at a conclusion about her meaning only to recoil on second thought with a perfectly verifiable conclusion that runs counter to the first and seems as valid. The difficulty in "pinning" her owes something to inadequate theoretical tools for interpreting narrative, something to sexist assumptions, something to the extraordinary complexity and achievement of her work; but the confusion is ours, not hers. The counterbalancing dip of one interpretation against another is basic to her message, which is far more capacious and consistent than any of the lesser messages she is seen either to support or to fall short of.

One of the most conspicuous and most damaging consequences of confusion in interpretation of her work has been the inadequate reading of her narrator. It has too often been assumed without much discussion that the narrator is the author, or that the narrator is a person, or that the narrator is an inadvertent effect. All of these assumptions lead to mistakes. The narrator can be considered as part of what she called the "rhythmic element" of her art; or as a Feuerbachian species-consciousness, not solely individual yet not transcendental but incarnate in the works of collective human minds and hands, past and present; or even as the power of collective memory. But whatever the interpretive venture in this case certain critical habits are simply inadequate for mature reading of this feature of her work. The narrator, for example, is most decidedly not a "mouthpiece" for the author, or worse, for Lewes, Comte, or Feuerbach; nor is her narrator the unconsidered result of a "psychological leak" on the author's part. The inadequacy of such interpretations becomes increasingly evident as the dimensions of George Eliot's achievement are grasped more fully.

Nineteen fifty-nine was an important year for George Eliot studies. Three fine books changed the drift and the tone of criticism toward a more analytic less thematic treatment of her art. The era of the backhanded compliment was not over, but it was put on notice by books from Barbara Hardy, Jerome Thale, and Reva Stump (each listed below). Gordon Haight's editions of her letters beginning in 1955, the republication that year of her translation of Feuerbach in an easily accessible edition, Thomas Pinney's collection of her essays in 1963, Gordon Haight's biography of 1968, and finally the publication in 1981 of her translation of Spinoza—all are scholarly events that have made more likely a fully informed estimate of her work.

Notes and References

Chapter One

1. John Cross reports this in his edition, *George Eliot's Life as Related in Her Letters and Journals*, 3 vols. (Edinburgh and London, 1885), 1:431, Mentioned by Gordon S. Haight in *George Eliot, A Biography* (New York and Oxford, 1968), 220.
2. Haight, *Biography*, 6. In this chapter I rely on Professor Haight's biography and on his edition of the letters; I rely in some places on others of the number of biographies available, but to date Haight's is the definitive work on her life.
3. Haight, *Biography*, 8.
4. Laetitia Cooper, *George Eliot: Writers and Their Works* (London, 1951), 10.
5. From *Scenes of Clerical Life*, "Janet's Repentence," chap. 10.
6. Cross, *Life*, 1:157.
7. *George Eliot Letters*, ed. Gordon S. Haight, 9 vols. (New Haven and London, 1955–78), 1:51. Future references to this edition will be included parenthetically in the text.
8. *Essays of George Eliot*, ed. Thomas Pinney (New York, 1963), 288. All future references to this edition will be included parenthetically in the text.
9. Haight, *Biography*, 38.
10. Ibid.,51.
11. Haight, *Biography*, 76.
12. Ibid., 123 and generally 96–123.
13. Ibid., 166. This view is characterized humorously as follows in chapter 1 of *Middlemarch*: "Sane people did what their neighbors did, so that if any lunatics were at large one could know and avoid them."
14. Lewes wrote to Chapman reflecting that "When *Jane Eyre* was finally known to be a woman's book [Charlotte Brontë's] the tone noticeably changed." *Letters*, 2:103.
15. Haight's phrase describing their arrival in Switzerland: "Their days in cheap lodgings were over." *Biography*, 293.
16. Haight, *Biography*, 355.

Chapter Two

1. Bernard Paris, "George Eliot and the Higher Criticism," *Anglia* 84 (1966): 69.

2. Ludwig Feuerbach, *The Essence of Christianity*, trans. George Eliot (New York, 1957), p. 64, book 1, ch. 5. All further references will be to this edition and will be included parenthetically in the text.

3. Commenting on Strauss in a letter, Marian Evans says, "the Galilean is nothing less than the genius of the future": a statement that reflects Strauss's tendency to make the Feuerbachian inversion that gives historical status to assertions about moral life once clothed in theological and dogmatic authority. *Letters*, 1:271.

4. *Essays*, 150. She is paraphrasing with evident approval the argument she is reviewing. The relation of ideas to things is an old philosophical issue. It is relevant to consider that George Eliot affirms the intention of this philosopher (Herr Gruppe) to depart from the profoundly influential philosophy of Emmanuel Kant, who distinguished the moral from the material world (as George Eliot does), but then within each distinguished a priori ideas from objects (George Eliot denies the validity of this distinction on the grounds that ideas are human constructs not transcendental realities and do not exist apart from their embodiments).

5. For further discussion of these issues and those in this section generally see Elizabeth Ermarth, "Incarnations: George Eliot's Conception of 'Undeviating Law,' " *Nineteenth-Century Fiction* 29, no. 3 (Dec.,1974); 273–86; and "George Eliot's Invisible Community," chap. 7 in *Realism and Consensus in the English Novel* (Princeton: Princeton University Press, 1983), especially the section on "Ideas and Things."

6. George Eliot's idea of culture differs somewhat from the idea of Matthew Arnold, whose discussions of the subject have been influential in nineteenth- and twentieth-century letters (see chap. 6).

7. *Middlemarch* (Boston: Houghton and Mifflin Riverside Edition, 1956), 61–62 (ch. 10).

8. "The realm of silence is large enough beyond the grave. This is the world of light and speech. . . ." *Letters*, 6:142.

9. Spinoza, *Ethics*, trans. George Eliot, ed. Thomas Deegan, Salzburg Studies in English Literature, no. 102.

10. Stuart Hampshire, *Spinoza* (New York: Penguin Books, 1951), see for example, 189, 209. In treating Spinoza I rely especially on this book and on the one by Karl Jaspers cited below, note 12.

11. Ibid., 80.

12. Karl Jaspers, *Spinoza*, vol. 2 of *The Great Philosophers*, ed. Hannah Arendt, trans. Ralph Manheim (New York and London: A Helen & Kurt Wolff Book, Harcourt Brace Jovanovich, 1957), 41.

13. Ibid., 44–45.

14. Ibid., 76–77.

15. Ibid., 82.

16. For further discussion see Hampshire, *Spinoza*, 125, and Feuerbach, *Essence*, viii.

17. Quoted in K. K. Collins, "Some Questions of Method: Some Unpublished Late Essays," *Nineteenth-Century Fiction* 35, no. 3 (December 1980): 387–88.

18. "Realism is thus the basis of all Art, and its antithesis is not Idealism, but *Falsism.*" George Henry Lewes, "Realism in Art: Recent German Fiction," *Westminster Review* 70 (1858): 493–96; often cited, and available in *Literary Criticism of George Henry Lewes*, ed. Alice R. Kaminsky (Lincoln: University of Nebraska Press, 1964), 89.

Chapter Three

1. "Evangelical Teaching: Dr. Cumming," in *Essays*, 166.
2. *Adam Bede* (New York: Holt, Rinehart, 1948), 178–82. All subsequent references will be to this edition and will be included parenthetically in the text.
3. "The Morality of Wilhelm Meister," in *Essays*, 147.
4. "The Antigone and Its Moral," in *Essays*, 264–65.
5. *Daniel Deronda*, ed. Barbara Hardy (Harmondsworth, England: Penguin, 1967), 583 (ch. 42).
6. "The Natural History of German Life," in *Essays*, 287; "The Influence of Rationalism," in *Essays*, 409. For a full discussion of this crucial point see Ermarth, "Incarnations," 273–86.
7. "The Influence of Rationalism," in *Essays*, 402.
8. In her review of *The Progress of the Intellect* she quotes from Mackay's "treasury": "The true religious philosophy of an imperfect being is not a system or creed, but, as Socrates thought, an infinite search or approximation. Finality is but another name for bewilderment or defeat. . . ." *Essays*, 44.
9. Carroll's remark is in "*Felix Holt:* Society as Protagonist," *Nineteenth-Century Fiction* 17 (1962); 238.
10. *Middlemarch*, 397 (ch. 54).
11. *Letters*, 2:134 and also 127. " 'Notre vraie destinée se compose de *resignation* et d'*activité* ' " (italics George Eliot's).
12. "Poetry and Prose from the Notebook of an Eccentric," in *Essays*, 17–19.
13. *Scenes of Clerical Life*, Foleshill Edition (Boston: Little, Brown & Co., 1910), "Amos Barton," 28 (ch. 2).
14. Invaluable treatments of Evangelicalism and its thorough influence on George Eliot's age are Ford K. Brown, *Fathers of the Victorians: The Age of Wilberforce* (Cambridge: Cambridge University Press, 1961), and Maurice J. Quinlan, *Victorian Prelude: A History of English Manners 1700–1830* (New York: Columbia University Press, 1941).
15. "The Natural History of German Life," in *Essays*, 270.
16. "Poetry and Prose from the Notebook of an Eccentric," in *Essays*, 15.

17. *Essays*, 446.
18. *The Mill on the Floss*, ed. Gordon S. Haight (Boston: Houghton Mifflin Riverside Edition, 1961), 244 (book 4, ch. 2). All subsequent references will be to this edition and will be included parenthetically in the text.
19. "The Natural History of German Life," in *Essays*, 282.
20. For further discussion of these issues see Elizabeth Ermarth, "Maggie Tulliver's Long Suicide," *Studies in English Literature* 14, no. 4 (Fall 1976); 587–601.
21. "Notes on Form in Art," in *Essays*, 433.

Chapter Four

1. *Essays*, 156.
2. *Letters*, 6:98.
3. *Essence*, pp. 122–23; ch. 12. Marian Evans's translation appeared in 1854; Feuerbach's work originally appeared in German in 1841.
4. *Essence*, pp. 158–59; ch. 16.
5. George Eliot quotes more than once this phrase from Comte: "Notre vraie destinée se compose de resignation et d'activité." See *Letters*, 3:127, 134.
6. To John Blackwood, 30 January 1877, *Letters*, 6:335.
7. *Romola* (New York: E. P. Dutton, Everyman Library, 1907), 524 (ch. 65). Subsequent references will be to this edition and will be included parenthetically in the text.
8. *Letters*, 3:392 (19 March 1861); 3:360 (28 November 1860).
9. *Silas Marner*, Foleshill Edition (Boston: Little, Brown and Co., 1910), 10, 44 (chs. 1, 5).
10. *Middlemarch*, 397 (ch. 54).
11. *Daniel Deronda* (Harmondsworth, England, 1967), 35–39 (ch. 1).
12. *Felix Holt, the Radical*, Foleshill Edition (Boston: Little, Brown and Co., 1910), 24, (ch. 1). All subsequent references will be to this edition and will be included parenthetically in the text.

Chapter Five

1. The phrase describes a similar situation in *Romola* (p. 99; ch. 9).
2. For Virginia Woolf's comment see *Times Literary Supplement*, 20 November 1919, 657–58; reprinted in *A Century of George Eliot Criticism*, ed. Gordon Haight (Boston, 1965).
3. *Middlemarch*, 13 (ch. 2). All subsequent references will be to this edition and will be included parenthetically in the text.
4. "The central unacted possibility" lies between Gwendolen and Deronda, according to Barbara Hardy, *The Novels of George Eliot* (New York, 1959), 148. It is important to remember, however, that it is only marriage that is unacted; friendship between them *is* enacted.

5. *Daniel Deronda*, 131 (ch. 9). All subsequent references will be to this edition and will be included parenthetically in the text.

6. F. R. Leavis's silly and ungenerous reading of *Daniel Deronda* in *The Great Tradition* deserves mention only because it has sponsored so much comment on the separability of the two inseparable plots.

7. See "The Future of German Philosophy," in *Essays*, 148–53. Thomas Vargish discusses the common denominator between the two plots in their demonstration of how ideas or mental anticipations get actualized, or, made incarnate ("George Eliot: Providence as Metaphor," chap. 4 in *The Providential Aesthetic in Victorian Fiction*, University of Virginia Press, 1985).

8. Avrom Fleishman, *Fiction and the Ways of Knowing* (Austin: University of Texas Press, 1978), 104–6.

Chapter Six

1. George Eliot congratulated Frederick Harrison on his article satirizing the essay that Arnold published in 1867 and that became part of the "Sweetness and Light" section of *Culture and Anarchy*. Her discussion of the "philistine," incidentally, preceded Arnold's by ten years; see *Essays*, 296–97.

2. U. C. Knoepflmacher, *George Eliot's Early Novels* (Berkeley and Los Angeles, 1968), 2.

3. C. B. Cox, *The Free Spirit: A Study of Liberal Humanism* (New York: Oxford University Press, 1963), 22–25; Marcia Midler, "George Eliot's Rebels: Portraits of the Artist as a Woman," *Women's Studies* 7 (1980); 97–108; Christopher Herbert, "Preachers and the Schemes of Nature in *Adam Bede*," *Nineteenth-Century Fiction* 29 (1975): 412–27; Carole Robinson, "*Romola*: A Reading of the Novel," *Victorian Studies* 6, no. 1 (Sept 1962): 29–42; Paul Bourl'honne, *George Eliot: Essai de Biographie* (Paris, Libraire Ancienne Honoré Champion, 1933); Laura Emery, *George Eliot's Creative Conflict* (Berkeley and Los Angeles: University of California Press, 1976), 14.

Selected Bibliography

The following list of critical books and articles is necessarily selective because of the large and increasing number of publications on George Eliot's work. This guide indicates the important directions in and contributions to George Eliot studies during the past fifty years. Guides to earlier research are also listed. I have tried to include mainly those critics who show signs of having come to terms with the central discussions, not by bibliographical overload but by intuitive sense and balance and by having done their homework; there are frequent signs in George Eliot studies that critics either do not cite or do not read each other's work, repeating excellent points made thirty years ago as if they were new discoveries. This is not a small problem for George Eliot because such work encourages circularity of discussion. The bibliography features criticism alive to central issues and to critical discussion. Three special issues (determinism, feminism, and the narrator) are listed separately because they have been so controversial and are so central. The bibliography is organized as follows: Primary Sources precede Secondary Sources; and the latter are divided into nine sections: (1) Biography; (2) Bibliography; (3) Critical Collections; (4) General Studies: Books; (5) General Studies: Articles and Chapters; (6–8) Special Issues (Determinism, Feminism, the Narrator) and (9) Studies of Individual Novels.

PRIMARY SOURCES

In the case of George Eliot's novels the entry is followed with a reference to the best currently available edition. Only a few of her most important essays are cited. Blackwood's Cabinet edition (1878) was the last one corrected by George Eliot and has been the standard edition. There has been no definitive edition of the novels, partly because textual problems with them have not appeared great and the need to establish texts not urgent. The Oxford Clarendon edition of the novels will be definitive, but so far only two volumes have appeared: *The Mill on the Floss*, edited by Gordon S. Haight (1980), and *Felix Holt, the Radical*, edited by Fred C. Thomson (1980).

"Poetry and Prose, from the Notebook of an Eccentric." Coventry *Herald and Observer*, 4 December 1846; 15 January 1847; 5, 12 and 19 February 1847. George Eliot's first published work apart from a short poem in 1840. (This essay is included, as are all the essays cited here, in Pinney's edition of the essays, cited below).

The Life of Jesus (Das Leben Jesu, 1835–36), by David Friedrich Strauss. 3 vols. London: Chapman Brothers, 1846. Translated anonymously from the fourth German edition.

Review of *The Progress of the Intellect*, by William Mackay. *Westminster Review* 54 (January 1851):353–68.*The Essence of Christianity (Das Wesen des Christenthums*, 1841), by Ludwig Feuerbach. Translated by Marian Evans. London: Chapman, 1854. Still the authoritative English translation, it was republished in the Harper Torchbook series (New York and London: Harper & Row, 1957) with an introduction by Karl Barth and a foreword by H. Richard Niebuhr.

"Woman in France: Madame de Sable." *Westminster Review* 62 (October 1854):448–73.*"*Evangelical Teaching: Dr. Cumming." *Westminster Review* 64 (October 1855):436–62.

"The Natural History of German Life." *Westminster Review* 66 (July 1856):51–79.

"Worldliness and Other-Worldliness: The Poet Young." *Westminster Review* 67 (January 1857):1–42.

Scenes of Clerical Life. 2 vols. Edinburgh and London: William Blackwood & Sons, 1858. Originally appeared serially in *Blackwood's Magazine*, January to October 1857. In addition to the Foleshill edition cited in the notes (Boston: Little, Brown & Co., 1910) there is the more easily accessible Penguin edition, edited by David Lodge, Harmondsworth, England, 1973.

Adam Bede. 3 vols. Edinburgh and London: William Blackwood & Sons, 1859. In addition to the Rinehart edition cited in the notes (New York: Holt, Rinehart, 1948), there is the more easily accessible Penguin edition, introduction by Stephen Gill, Harmondsworth, England, 1980.

The Mill on the Floss. 3 vols. Edinburgh and London: William Blackwood & Sons, 1860. Besides the new Clarendon edition (1980) there is the more readily available Riverside edition by Gordon S. Haight cited in the notes (Boston: Houghton Mifflin Co., 1961).

Silas Marner. Edinburgh and London: William Blackwood & Sons, 1861. Penguin edition, Harmondsworth, England, 1968.

Romola. 3 vols. London: Smith, Elder & Co., 1863. Originally appeared serially in *Cornhill Magazine* July 1862 to August 1863. In addition to the Everyman addition cited in the notes (New York: E. P. Dutton, 190), there is the more easily accessible Penguin edition edited by Andrew Sanders, Harmondsworth, England, 1980.

"The Influence of Rationalism." *Fortnightly Review* 1 (15 May 1865):43–55.
Felix Holt, the Radical. 3 vols. Edinburgh and London: William Blackwood
& Sons, 1866. Besides the new Clarendon edition (1980) there is the
Foleshill edition cited in the notes (Boston: Little, Brown & Co., 1910)
and the more readily available Penguin edition edited by Peter Cove-
ney, Harmondsworth, England, 1972.
The Spanish Gypsy. Edinburgh and London: William Blackwood & Sons,
1868. Available in Cabinet and other complete editions of her work, as
are other poems she published during this time: "How Lisa Loved the
King" (*Blackwoods Magazine*, 5 May 1869), "Brother and Sister" son-
nets, "Agatha" (*Atlantic Monthly*, August 1869), "The Legend of Jubal"
(*Macmillans Magazine*, May 1870), "Armgart" (*Macmillans Magazine*,
July 1871).
Middlemarch, a Study of Provincial Life. 4 vols. Edinburgh and London: Wil-
liam Blackwood & Sons, 1872; and 1 vol., 1874 originally appeared in
eight parts, 1871–72. Riverside edition, edited by Gordon S. Haight
(Boston: Houghton Mifflin Co., 1956).
The Legend of Jubal and other Poems. Edinburgh and London: William Black-
wood & Sons, 1874.
Daniel Deronda. 4 Vols Edinburgh and London: William Blackwood & Sons,
1876. Originally appeared in eight parts between February and Septem-
ber 1876. Penguin edition, edited by Barbara Hardy, Harmondsworth,
England, 1967.
The Impressions of Theophrastus Such. Edinburgh and London: William Blackwood & Sons, 1879. Available in Cabinet and other complete editons.
Essays of George Eliot. Edited by Thomas Pinney, New York: Columbia University Press, 1963.
Ethics (Ethica Ordine Geometrico Demonstrata, published in *Opera Posthuma*,
1677), by Benedict de Spinoza. Translated by George Eliot. Edited by
Thomas Deegan. Salzburg Studies in English Literature, no. 102. Salzburg: Unstitut für Anglistik und Amerikanistik, 1981.The first publication of George Eliot's translation and a crucial resource for any scholar
working on George Eliot (always keeping in mind the cautions discussed above, chap. two).
George Eliot: A Writer's Notebook 1854–1879, and Uncollected Writings. Edited
by Joseph Wiesenfarth. Charlottesville: University of Virginia Press,
1981. Published for the Bibliographical Society of the University of
Virginia.Unlike some of the more specialized notebooks this one covers
a long period and thus gives a clear idea of some important emphases:
for example, her continuous interest in the condition of women (see her
early entries on Egyptian women; her note that Petrarch is a "bitter mi-
sogynist"); her early and abiding habit of research and reading for all
her novels, not just *Romola* and Daniel Deronda; her functional knowl-

edge of languages; and even confirmation that her best poetry was the epigrammatic, satiric sort. Contains a useful bibliography.

1. Letters and Diaries
George Eliot's Life as Related in Her Letters and Journals. 3 vols. Edited by John Walter Cross. London: William Blackwood & Sons; New York: Harper & Brothers, 1885.
George Eliot and John Chapman, with John Chapman's Diaries. Edited by Gordon S. Haight. New Haven and London: Yale University Press, 1940. Containing more of Chapman than of George Eliot, this first volume from her twentieth-century editor and biographer attempts to restore the real George Eliot by presenting the correspondence with Chapman that Cross had virtually eliminated; but in erasing an old distortion he institutes a new one, that of the dependent George Eliot, citing the phrenologist Combe's preposterous diagnosis ("She was not fitted to stand alone") as a keynote (Haight used it forty years later as the motto for his *Biography*).
George Eliot Letters. Edited By Gordon S. Haight. 9 vols. New Haven and London: Yale University Press, 1954–78. Scrupulous and informative, this definitive edition of her letters is essential reading.

SECONDARY SOURCES

1. Biography
The definitive biography is Gordon S. Haight's. Others have been listed as useful because each offers a new angle on the author and thus a reminder that the biographical record is often opaque or inconclusive. The best places to begin getting a sense of the author are still the invaluable editions of her letters and of her essays.

Bullett, Gerald. *George Eliot: Her Life and Books.* London: Collins, 1947. Includes brief excerpts from the letters, Strauss, Feuerbach, and Lewes, as well as some literary interpretation. Historically important for its focus on central issues and its partial refusal to accept the stereotyped view of George Eliot as the novelist of duty without pleasure; since superceded as biography by Haight's.
Cooper, Lettice. *George Eliot: Writers and Their Works.* London and New York: Longmans Green & Co., 1951 (44 pp.). Short, spirited biographical sketch including interpretations of the fiction; repudiates implicitly the critical distortions of the period since George Eliot's death.
Haight, Gordon S. *George Eliot, A Biography.* Oxford and New York: Oxford University Press, 1968. The definitive biography; scrupulous in its

refusal to speculate or to make a coherent narrative where the record
does not warrant it.

Redinger, Ruby. *George Eliot: The Emergent Self.* New York: Alfred A.
Knopf, 1975. Attempts the speculative unity that Haight resists,
though the speculation is not always acknowledged as such; falls into
clichés when interpreting the fiction. Readable but does not add much
to Haight's picture.

2. Bibliographical Guides

Harvey, W. J. "George Eliot." In *Victorian Fiction: A Guide to Research,* edited by Lionel Stevenson. Cambridge, Mass.: Harvard University Press,
1964. Includes good summary of two "stereotyped attitudes" to George
Eliot.

Marshall, William H. "A Selective Bibliography of Writings about George
Eliot, to 1965," *Bulletin of Bibliography* 25, nos. 3–4 (1967):70–72,
88–94.

Fulmer, Constance Marie. *George Eliot: A Reference Guide.* Boston: G. K.
Hall & Co., 1977. Covers the period from 1858 through 1971; many
entries annotated.

Knoepflmacher, U. C. "George Eliot." In *Victorian Fiction: A Second Guide
to Research,* edited by George Ford. New York: Modern Language Association of America, 1978. Covers the period from 1963 through 1974.
Includes valuable caution concerning the "superfluity" of articles that
overlap or rephrase previous discussion (sometimes without acknowledgment).

Higdon, David Leon. "A Bibliography of George Eliot Criticism 1971–
1977." *Bulletin of Bibliography* 37, no. 2 (Spring–June 1980):90–103.

3. General Critical Collections

Carroll, David R. *George Eliot: The Critical Heritage.* New York: Barnes &
Noble, 1971. Collection of contemporary reviews with a splendid introduction outlining her contemporary reception.

Creeger, George, ed. *George Eliot: A Collection of Critical Essays.* Englewood
Cliffs, N.J.: Prentice-Hall, 1970. Consistently good collection of arti-
cles published in various journals between 1954 and 1966, including
"George Eliot's Religion of Humanity," by Bernard Paris; "The Au-
thority of the Past in George Eliot's Novels," by Thomas Pinney; "The
Moment of Disenchantment in George Eliot's Novels," by Barbara
Hardy; "George Eliot's Conception of Form," by Darrel Mansell;
"George Eliot, Feuerbach and the Question of Criticism," by U. C.
Knoepflmacher, as well as some interpretations of novels.

Haight, Gordon S., ed. *A Century of George Eliot Criticism.* Boston: Houghton Mifflin, 1965. Selections from critical essays published between
1858 and 1962. Complementary with Carroll.

Hardy, Barbara, comp. *Critical Essays on George Eliot.* New York: Barnes & Noble, 1970. Uneven collection, partly because of focus on the opposition between the "picture" and "diagram" in George Eliot's work, an opposition that begs important questions.

Knoepflmacher, U. C., and George Levine, guest eds. *George Eliot, 1880–1980.* Special George Eliot issue of *Nineteenth-Century Fiction* 35, no. 3 (December 1980). Various centenary essays including ones on George Eliot's positive influence for women (Elaine Showalter), and on George Eliot's restrained relationship to positivism (K. K. Collins and Martha Vogeler).

Smith, Anne, ed. *George Eliot: Centennary Essays and an Unpublished Fragment.* New York: Barnes & Noble, 1980. Discussions of central issues, combines intellectual sophistication with often weak scholarship; no mention made of many valuable prior discussions of these issues, thus falsely implying new discovery and aggravating the circular tendency in George Eliot studies.

4. General Studies: Books

Bennett, Joan. *George Eliot, Her Mind and Art.* Cambridge: Cambridge University Press, 1948. An early and still sound discussion; alive to central issues and usually sound in interpretation; alert to George Eliot's feminism though like the author does not use the term.

Hardy, Barbara. *The Novels of George Eliot.* New York: Oxford University Press, 1959. Important and influential study, instrumental in turning the tide of discussion away from George Eliot as purveryor of moral lessons to George Eliot as artist. Various essays treat the novels in sequence and open avenues for interpreting plot, narrative voice, style; includes the splendid chapter on "Possibilities." Essential reading.

Harvey, W. J. *The Art of George Eliot.* London: Chatto & Windus, 1963. Excellent first chapter on George Eliot and the criticism of fiction dealing with the infancy of the latter and its distortion of the former. Brings into relief the technical fineness of George Eliot's work: sensitive readings but not reliable on theoretical subjects such as her views of time, or her narrative method.

Jones, R. T. *George Eliot.* Cambridge: Cambridge University Press, 1970. Textual interpretation that allegedly eschews all background study; perceptive readings of all the major narratives except *Romola*, which is omitted for unconvincing reasons.

Knoepflmacher, U. C. *George Eliot's Early Novels: The Limits of Realism.* Berkeley and Los Angeles: University of California Press, 1968. An influential statement of the position that realism and moral vision are at odds in George Eliot, a view with which the present study plainly disagrees. Draws attention to important issues, offers locally perceptive insights, and frustratingly wrongheaded conclusions of the sort common in works that emphasize a Victorian intellectual background, and take George Eliot to be more typical than she is.

Leavis, F. R. *The Great Tradition: George Eliot, Henry James, Joseph Conrad.* London: Chatto & Windus, 1948. With friends like this George Eliot scarcely needs enemies. Concerned with sensibility, Leavis is often seen as an important force in restoring George Eliot's reputation: a testimony to the low state of George Eliot criticism in 1948. Leavis most notoriously discards half of *Daniel Deronda* as weak and unnecessary, and subsequently the novel has endured far too many discussions prompted by this flashy but often silly essay.

Milner, Ian. *The Structure of Values in George Eliot.* Prague: Universita Karlova, 1968.

Paris, Bernard J. *Experiments in Life: George Eliot's Quest for Values.* Detroit: Wayne State University Press, 1965. Substantial but strained discussion of George Eliot's philosophical position. Shows the importance of Feuerbach, but overschematizes the influence of positivism. Emphasizes mercilessly and distortingly various binary oppositions such as realism versus moralism, objectivity versus subjectivity, truth versus value.

Pearce. T. S. *George Eliot.* Totowa, N.J.: Rowman & Littlefield, 1973. Excellent short book on her life, times, and works. Valuable particular observations on novels.

Stump, Reva. *Movement and Vision in George Eliot's Novels.* Seattle: University of Washington Press, 1959. Intelligent and suggestive discussion of the relation between metaphors of vision and the rhythmic movement toward and away from moral insight. Deals with *Adam Bede, The Mill on the Floss,* and *Middlemarch.* Apologetic tone of preface belies the toughness of intellectual achievement.

Thale, Jerome. *The Novels of George Eliot.* New York and London: Columbia University Press, 1959. Still one of the best books on George Eliot, the interpretations of individual works are sensitive, suggestive, and intelligent.

Witemeyer, Hugh. *George Eliot and the Visual Arts.* New Haven and London: Yale University Press, 1979. Careful discussion of George Eliot's use of pictorial traditions in her fiction.

5. General Studies: Articles and Chapters
    In addition to Beer, Ermarth, Levine, and Mansell (under Special Issues) see also:

Buckler, William. "Memory, Morality, and the Tragic Vision in the Early Novels of George Eliot." In *The English Novel in the Nineteenth Century,* edited by George Goodin. Urbana: University of Illinois Press, 1972.

Ermarth, Elizabeth. "George Eliot's Invisible Community." In her *Realism and Consensus in the English Novel,* pp. 222–56. Princeton: Princeton University Press, 1983. Discusses the power of memory, the identity between ideas and things, and the unifying collective narrative consciousness in her novels; particular discussion of *Adam Bede* and *Middlemarch*.

Feltes, Norman. "George Eliot and the Unified Sensibility." *PMLA* 79, no. 1 (March 1964):130–36. Suggestive treatment of George Eliot's conscious effort to unite the dissociated sensibility.

Gezari, Janet. "The Metaphorical Imagination of George Eliot." *ELH* 45, no. 1 (Spring 1978):93–106. Good discussion of George Eliot's language and the activity it engenders in readers.

Hurley, Edward. "Death and Immortality: George Eliot's Solution." *Nineteenth-Century Fiction* 24, no. 2 (September 1969):222–27. Brief discussion of how history, tradition, and the past constitute a new basis for immortality.

Levine, George. "George Eliot's Hypothesis of Reality." *Nineteenth-Century Fiction* 35, no 1 (June 1980):1–28. Consciousness, fusing ideal and real, establishes a continuum in experience that would otherwise be dissociated. Relies considerably on Lewes's writing rather than George Eliot's to gain access to this point but usually accurate in drawing inferences.

Paris, Bernard J. "George Eliot and the Higher Criticism." *Anglia* 84, no. 1 (1966):59–73. Important article on George Eliot's philosophical position, despite a distracting habit of schematizing ("George Eliot the positivist," "George Eliot the pantheist"); important for distinction between the "transcendental spirit" of Strauss and Hegel on the one hand and George Eliot's Feuerbachian emphasis on the concrete and particular.

Vargish, Thomas. "George Eliot: Providence as Metaphor." In his *The Providential Aesthetic in Victorian Fiction,* pp. 163–243. Charlottesville: University of Virginia Press, 1985. Important discussion of how George Eliot's usage transforms a major fictional convention. (Introduction on the Providential Aesthetic also useful.) Deals with all the novels.

Witemeyer, Hugh. "George Eliot and Jean-Jacques Rousseau." *Comparative Literature Studies* 16, no. 2 (June 1979):121–30. Useful discussion of an important influence on George Eliot.

Wright, T. R. "George Eliot and Positivism: A Reassessment." *Modern Language Review* 76, no. 2 (Spring 1981):257–72. Important step in estimating the limits of George Eliot's allegiance to Comte, but not the last; shows she anticipated Comte to some degree and took a friendly but not evangelical interest in him; that he prompted her thought but did not direct it. See also K. K. Collins and Martha Vogeler in Knoepflmacher and Levine, eds., George Eliot special issue (cited above).

Zimmerman, Bonnie. " 'Radiant as a Diamond': George Eliot, Jewelery, and the Female Role." *Criticism* 19, no 3 (Summer 1977):212–22. Demonstrates George Eliot's controlled use of detail.

6. Special Issues: Determinism

Beer, Gillian. "Beyond Determinism: George Eliot and Virginia Woolf."
In *Women Writing and Writing About Women*, edited by Mary Jacobus,
pp. 80–100. New York: Barnes & Noble, 1979. Excellent discussion
of the idea of determinism, its relatively modern nature, its implications for plot, and the conscious resistance to those implications by two
major women writers.

Ermarth, Elizabeth. "Incarnations: George Eliot's Conception of 'Undeviating Law.' " *Nineteenth-Century Fiction* 29, no. 3 (December
1974):273–86. The radical separation of culture and nature in George
Eliot, preserving a realm of freedom in which ideas and things are one,
has radical implications for her idea of determinism; the objects of culture are embodied ideas, each a "law" but submitting to no teleological
system.

Levine, George. "Determinism and Responsibility." *PMLA* 77, no. 2 (June
1962):268–79; also in Haight, *Century of Criticism*. That George Eliot's
determinism is not inconsistent with and is even essential to her emphasis on moral responsibility. Excellent.

7. Special Issues: Feminism

Austen, Zelda. "Why Feminist Critics are Angry with George Eliot." *Col-
lege English* 37, no. 6 (February 1976):549–61. Excellent summary of
critical discussion and perceptive interpretation of George Eliot's position on women; that it is a most powerful feminist act to show the limits of sanctioned norms.

Blake, Kathleen. "*Middlemarch* and the Woman Question." *Nineteenth-Century Fiction* 31, no. 3 (December 1976): 285–312. How George Eliot's
central issues are women's issues; the ontological disaster of having no
active place hounds her heroines. Ably illuminates both George Eliot
and the sexist strain in past interpretations of her.

Ermarth, Elizabeth. "Maggie Tulliver's Long Suicide." *Studies in English
Literature* 14, no. 4 (Fall 1974):587–601. That Maggie internalizes the
sexist norms of her family and thus learns to destroy herself.

Pell, Nancy. "The Fathers' Daughters in *Daniel Deronda*." *Nineteenth-Century
Fiction* 36, no. 4 (March 1982):424–51. Forceful demonstration that
the two plots are unified by their "destructive patriarchal organization."
Useful bibliographical references; flirts with distorting biographical
speculation.

Gilbert, Sandra, and Susan Gubar. *The Madwoman in the Attic*. New Haven and London: Yale University Press, 1979. It must be said, because
of this otherwise-good book's wide currency, that among its many virtues is not an informed discussion of George Eliot. Quotations are mis-
leadingly or wrongly ascribed, previous discussion often goes unac-
knowledged, and many statements are demonstrably false (it is simply

false, for example, to say that in George Eliot intellectual deprivation nourishes emotional life; quite the contrary.) Such problems suggest a distance from George Eliot's work that permits bending her to support a thesis that she does not fit.

Sedgwick, Eve Kosofsky. *"Adam Bede* and *Henry Esmond:* Homosocial Desire and the Historicity of the Female." In her *Between Men: English Literature and Male Homosocial Desire.* New York: Columbia University Press, 1985. Provocative discussion of the intimacy between gender arrangements and economic division. Better on theoretical issues (see her Introduction) than on *Adam Bede.*

Showalter, Elaine. *A Literature of Their Own.* Princeton: Princeton University Press, 1977. George Eliot sections redress a balance by showing George Eliot's positive influence on women writers.

8. Special Issues: The Narrator

Anderson, Quentin. "George Eliot in *Middlemarch."* In his *From Dickens to Hardy,* 274–93. Vol. 6 of *Pelican Guide to English Literature,* Harmondsworth: Penguin Books, 1958; also in Haight, *Century of Criticism.* Illustrative example of approaches to her narrator until recently, this essay offers perceptive comments about the narrator's effect together with complete absence of distinction between the narrator and the author, and some breath-taking condescension.

Armstrong, Isobel. *"Middlemarch:* A Note on George Eliot's Wisdom." In *Critical Essays on George Eliot,* edited by Barbara Hardy. New York: Barnes & Noble, 1970. George Eliot's narrator is a deliberate construction with particular features.

Dowden, Edward. "George Eliot." In *Century of George Eliot Criticism,* edited by Gordon S. Haight, pp. 64–73. Boston: Houghton Mifflin, 1965. Early and still useful treatment of the narrator as distinct from the author: a "second self" set apart as a separate entity with particular characteristics.

Ermarth, Elizabeth. "Method and Moral in George Eliot's Narrative." *Victorian Newsletter,* no. 47 (Spring 1975):4–8. That the medium is the message in George Eliot, and that one feature of the medium is the narrator's lack of omniscience.

Mansell, Darrel. "Ruskin and George Eliot's Realism." *Criticism* 7 (Summer 1965):203–16. The importance of subjectivity to the fully objective picture of reality in both authors.

Martin, Graham. *"The Mill on the Floss* and the Unreliable Narrator." In *George Eliot: Centenary Essays and an Unpublished Fragment,* edited by Anne Smith. New York: Barnes & Noble, 1980. Often wrong-headed but provocative essay on the contradictions in the narrative voice, and between that voice and its story.

156 GEORGE ELIOT

Miller, J. Hillis. "The Narrator as General Consciousness." In his *The Form of Victorian Fiction*. Notre Dame: University of Notre Dame Press, 1968. Suggestive lecture on the narrator in George Eliot and other Victorian novelists.

Newton, K. M. "The Role of the Narrator in George Eliot's Novels." *Journal of Narrative Technique* 3, no. 2 (May 1973):97–107. Excellent discussion posing many of the interesting questions about George Eliot's narrators and showing the limits of previous criticism on the subject.

Oldfield, Derek. "The Language of the Novel: The Character of Dorothea." In *Middlemarch: Critical Approaches*, edited by Barbara Hardy, pp. 63–86. New York: Oxford University Press, 1967. Traces the "zig-zag" activity of consciousness as it is directed by the language of the novel. Not explicitly about the narrator, but implicitly so.

9. Individual Works

In addition to the following, there are discussions of individual novels in the works cited above under General Studies by Bennett, Ermarth, Hardy, Pearce, Jones, Stump, and Thale. *Scenes of Clerical Life* still awaits thorough study.

a. *Adam Bede*

Adam, Ian. "The Structure of Realisms in *Adam Bede*." *Nineteenth-Century Fiction* 30, no. 2 (September 1975):127–49. Excellent discussion of the temporal and spatial habits of the novel; shows how the narrative voice mediates and unifies the dual worlds of the novel.

Creeger, George. "An Interpretation of *Adam Bede*." *ELH* 23, no. 3 (September 1956):218–38; also in Creeger, *Critical Essays*. The conflict between two ways of life linked by a central process of redemption.

Gregor, Ian. "The Two Worlds of *Adam Bede*." In *The Moral and The Story*, by Ian Gregor and Brian Nichols, pp. 13–32. London: Faber & Faber, 1962. An influential essay, this focuses on the dual worlds of comfortably idyll and of struggling sorrow. Discussion so good that its conclusion (that George Eliot was confusing genres) seems outlandish.

Harvey, W. J. "The Treatment of Time in *Adam Bede*." *Anglia* 75 (1957):429–40; also in Haight, *Century of Criticism*. Problematic but suggestive effort to show how the narrator (he says the novelist) suppresses the causal relations that underlie the plot, diverting attention from temporal processes; draws the unjustified conclusion that George Eliot does this because she is unable to face the implications of what he calls her determinism.

Squires, Michael. "*Adam Bede* and the *Locus Amoenus*." *Studies in English Literature* 13, no 4 (Autumn 1973):670–76. Demonstrates that George Eliot uses classical topoi; a useful reminder of the invisible and manifold ways her knowledge shapes her art, though he, too, feels compelled to wonder whether she knew what she was doing.

b. *The Mill on the Floss*

In addition to Ermarth (under Special Issues: Feminism), see also:

Hagan, John. "A Re-Interpretation of *The Mill on the Floss.*" *PMLA* 87, no. 1 (January 1972):53–63. Summarizes criticism and restates some central issues.

Paris, Bernard J. "The Conflicts of Maggie Tulliver: A Horneyan Analysis." *Centennial Review* 12 (1968–69):166–99. Applies Karen Horney's theories of neurosis with illuminating results despite unsupported biographical speculation about and condescension to George Eliot who is seen as not intending her main effects; sees the consistency in Maggie's actions.

Putzell, Sara. "An Antagonism of Valid Claims: The Dynamics of *The Mill on the Floss.*" *Studies in the Novel* (North Texas State) 7, (1975):227–44.

Steig, Michael. "Anality in *The Mill on the Floss.*" *Novel* 5, no. 1 (Fall 1971):42–53. Unfortunate title notwithstanding (he sees George Eliot's treatment of the Dodsons as an anticipation of Freud's description of "anal" personalities), this discussion is alive to the contradictions George Eliot presents in Maggie's character, and to their basis in the social fact that she is a woman.

c. *Silas Marner*

Carroll, David R. "*Silas Marner*: Reversing the Oracles of Religion." *Literary Monographs,* 1:165–200. Madison, Milwaukee and London: University of Wisconsin Press, 1967. The two plots represent two ways of approaching the central problems of meaning the work raises. Splendidly argued and valuable not only for *Silas* but for general insight into George Eliot's literary habits.

Milner, Ian. "Structure and Quality in *Silas Marner.*" *Studies in English Literature* 16, no. 4 (Autumn 1966):717–29. Double plot reinforces class division; the central imperative is to transcend such division.

Swann, Brian. "*Silas Marner* and the New Mythus." *Criticism* 18, no. 2 (Spring 1976): 101–21. Valuable discussions of the creativity of human consciousness in George Eliot and of its independence from nature; intelligent use of Comte and Feuerbach garnished with unfortunate biographical speculation.

d. *Romola*

Hurley, Edward. "Piero di Cosimo: An Alternate Analogy for George Eliot's Realism." *Victorian Newsletter*, no. 31 (Spring 1967):54–58. That the imaginatively venturesome Piero is a better model for her art than the Dutch realists.

Poston, Lawrence. "Setting and Theme in *Romola.*" *Nineteenth-Century Fiction* 20, no. 4 (March 1966):355–66. The Florentine Renaissance setting helps George Eliot comment on the intimacy of the public and the private life: illuminating and suggestive.

Sullivan, William J. "Piero di Cosimo and the Higher Primitivism in *Romola*." *Nineteenth-Century Fiction* 26, no. 4 (March 1972):390–405. A real historical figure, though a minor character, Piero provides important perspective on the philosophical and moral values of Renaissance Florence; excellent.

Wilt, Judith. *Ghosts of the Gothic*. Princeton: Princeton University Press, 1980. George Eliot section, especially on *Romola*, has interesting general discussion of the exercise of consciousness in George Eliot's novels; tends, like other discussions of the fabulous in George Eliot, to overstate its importance by neglecting the historical dimension of her work.

e. *Felix Holt*

Carroll, David R. "*Felix Holt*: Society as Protagonist." *Nineteenth-Century Fiction* 17, no. 3 (December 1962):237–52; also in Creeger, *Critical Essays*. Good discussion of balance between the individual and the social, and of analogies between love, politics, and religion; includes the misleading view that conflict in George Eliot is a sign of social breakdown.

Edwards, Michael. "George Eliot and Negative Form." *Critical Quarterly* 17, no. 2 (Summer 1975):171–79. Excellent discussion of George Eliot's formal sophistication, and of limits of earlier reductive of dismissive criticism.

Horowitz, Lenore. "George Eliot's Vision of Society in *Felix Holt, the Radical*." *Texas Studies in Literature and Language* 17, no. 1 (Spring 1975):175–91. Reliable discussion of novel's emphasis on historical change in a hierarchical society, and on the relations between social outsiders and insiders.

f. *Middlemarch*: Books and Critical Collections

Adam, Ian. ed. *This Particular Web: Essays on Middlemarch*. Toronto and Buffalo: University of Toronto Press, 1975. Excellent collection of essays by Barbara Hardy, Gordon Haight, U. C. Knoepflmacher, David Carroll, and Gillian Beer.

Beaty, Jerome. *Middlemarch from Notebook to Novel*. Urbana: University of Illinois Press, 1960. Based on Anna Kitchell's publication of the *Middlemarch* notebooks; detailed comparisons of the notebooks and manuscript revisions of the novel. Corrected the once-current superstition that George Eliot wrote by spontaneous overflow rather than by careful planning, writing, and revising.

Hardy, Barbara, ed. *Middlemarch: Critical Approaches to the Novel*. New York: Oxford University Press, 1967. Contains valuable essays on the novel's intellectual background and contemporary reception (W. J. Harvey), its textual variants (Jerome Beaty), its narrative structure and language (Mark Schorer, Derek Oldfield, Hilda Hulme), the incarnate nature of its form (Barbara Hardy), and the dangers of schematic criticism (J. M. S. Tompkins).

Kitchell, Anna T., ed. *George Eliot's Quarry for "Middlemarch."* Berkeley and Los Angeles: University of California Press, 1950. George Eliot's notes and plans for the novel.

g. *Middlemarch:* Articles
In addition to Armstrong and Blake (under Special Issues) see also:

Ashton, Rosemary. "The Intellectual 'Medium' of *Middlemarch.*" *Review of English Studies,* n.s. 30, no. 118 (May 1979):154–68. Interesting attempt to trace the influence of George Eliot's intellectual inheritance from Comte, Strauss, Spinoza, and Feuerbach in the language of the novel.

Hardy, Barbara. "*Middlemarch:* Public and Private Worlds." *English* 25, no. 121 (Spring 1976):5–26. That the novels emphasize the public result of private statement or gesture; the importance of historical imagination; corroboration of George Eliot's "sharply feminist consciousness."

Hollahan, Eugene. "The Concept of 'Crisis' in *Middlemarch.*" *Nineteenth-Century Fiction* 28, no. 4 (March 1974):450–57. Conventional list of the novel's "crises" informed by sensible exposition of Ladislaw as a key figure in uniting in himself his scattered powers, and in urging the same result in others.

Kiely, Robert. "The Limits of Dialogue in *Middlemarch.*" In *The Worlds of Victorian Fiction,* edited by Jerome Buckley, pp. 103–23. Cambridge, Mass. and London: Harvard University Press, 1975. Excellent essay on the social dimensions of language in George Eliot; clear and accessible interpretation of the "interrupted dialectic" as a characteristic structure of experience in the novel; takes one scene as an emblem for more massively orchestrated method in the novel.

Knoepflmacher, U. C. "*Middlemarch:* An Avuncular View." *Nineteenth-Century Fiction* 30, no. 1 (June 1975):53–81. That the novel sustains a critique of patriarchal values evidenced in the relation of male guardians (uncles) to their female wards; the almost total default of these guardians for the wards and for society at large.

Lyons, Richard S. "The Method of *Middlemarch.*" *Nineteenth-Century Fiction* 21, no. 1 (June 1966):35–47. Demonstrates how the undertones of thought function in the novel; focuses on chapter 39 and traces resonances from that point.

Miller, J. Hillis. "Optic and Semiotic in *Middlemarch.*" In *The Worlds of Victorian Fiction,* edited by Jerome Buckley, pp. 125–45. Cambridge, Mass. and London: Harvard University Press, 1975. That the novel shows each of a series of "totalizing" metaphors being met with inevitable limitation, each absolute picture being relativized; goes too far, however, in concluding that these "cancel" each other's claims to validity.

h. *Daniel Deronda*
    In addition to Pell (under Special Issues: Feminism), see also:
Beer, Gillian. "Descent and Sexual Selection: Women in Narrative." In her
    *Darwin's Plots: Evolutionary Narrative in Darwin, George Eliot, and Nine-
    teenth-Century Fiction.* London: Routledge and Kegan Paul, 1983. The
    dysteleological elements in *Daniel Deronda* especially concerning Gwen-
    dolen's problem in learning to accept indeterminacy.
Fast, Robin Riley. "Getting to the Ends of *Daniel Deronda.*" *Journal of Nar-
    rative Technique* 7, (1977):200–17. Excellent discussion of the differing
    methods and motives of the two plots.
Fleishman, Avrom. "Daniel Charisi." In his *Fiction and the Ways of Know-
    ing.* Austin: University of Texas Press, 1978. Treats the central prob-
    lem of community; excellent discussion of the "Jewish half" as equal to
    the Gwendolen half, posing different but homologous problems.
Gottfried, Leon. "Structure and Genre in *Daniel Deronda.*" In *The English
    Novel in the Nineteenth Century*, edited by George Goodin, pp. 164–75.
    Urbana: University of Illinois Press, 1972. A bit simple on the genre
    relations of novel and romance, but sees that the two plots are mediated
    by both central characters. Notable for valiant stand against condescen-
    sion: "As a part of the respect we owe a great novelist we should judge
    her art as art, even when it does not altogether succeed, and not as a
    slow leak in her subconscious."
Kearney, John. "Time and Beauty in *Daniel Deronda.*" *Nineteenth-Century
    Fiction* 26, no. 3 (December 1971):286–306. Suggestive reading of
    Gwendolen's need for ideas in order to develop a character; less good on
    the "Jewish half."

Index

Activity, in Spinoza, 37–38; *see* Resignation
Adam Bede, 16, 54–55, 68–77; perspective in, 70
Arnold, Matthew, 134–35, 142n6, 145n1
Art, as surprise, 41, 61; difference as form in, 42, 88, 92–93, 127; life as, 39, 86, 88; relation to sympathy, 107; vocation as 59–60, 135–36; *see* Culture, and individual creativity; freedom from nature (artificiality of); *see* Differences

Blackwood, John, 15, 93
Bodichon, Barbara (*née,* Leigh-Smith), 9, 17
Brabant, Rufa (Mrs. Charles Hennell), 6
Bray, Cara (*née,* Caroline Hennell), 5; refuge with, 7–8
Bray, Charles, 4–5, 26

Chapman, John, 8, 13, 14
Combe, George, 11–12, 149
Community, and culture, 134; failure of in *The Mill on the Floss,* 77–79; implied in *Middlemarch,* 111–12; in *Daniel Deronda,* 128–31; in Milby, 60–66; recognition of in *Adam Bede,* 74–76; *see* Narrative voice
Concreteness, of what is general, 55–57; principle of individuation and, 56
Confession, defined, 121; in *Adam Bede,* 109; in *Daniel Deronda,* 109, 127; in "Janet's Repentance," 66
Conflict, of valid claims, 56, 135; in *The Mill on the Floss,* 77–78, 80–81, 86–88; in *Romola,* 95–97; positive value of, 57–58
Cross, John Walter, 21, 23–24; and George Eliot's reputation, 137

Culture, and individual creativity, 30, 31–32, 133–35; and science, 31–32; and tradition, 30–31, 53–58, 71; as incarnation, 56–57; freedom from nature (artificiality of), 30, 53–54, 66–67, 69, 133

D'Albert Durade, Francois, 7, 77
Daniel Deronda, 22, 99, 101, 109–10, 121–31
Desire, importance of in *Middlemarch,* 113–14; for individual creativity, *see* Culture, and individual creativity
Determinism, objections to, 58; *see* Incarnation
Development of George Eliot's art, 63, 99–100, 102, 106–7, 109–10, 136
Differences, Feuerbach on, 91–93; and art—*see* Art, difference as form in

Essays, 39–52; on art, 39–42; on "Evangelical Teaching: Dr. Cumming," 45–47; on "The Influence of Rationalism," 51; on "The Natural History of German Life," 47–49, 79; on "Progress of the Intellect," 44–45; on women, 42–44; on "Worldliness and Other-Worldliness: The Poet Young," 49–51; summary of themes in, 51–52
Evangelicalism, 2, 65, 143n6
External reason, 57–58

Felix Holt, the Radical, 21, 99, 101–7
Feuerbach, Ludwig, *Das Wesen des Christentums,* 1841 [*The Essence of Christianity,* trans. Marian Evans, 1856], 11, 25–32; main point of, 29; method of, 25–28; on cognizance of species, 28, 68; sympathy and, 90–93, 127, 139–40, 142n3

Freedom, culture and, 53; George Eliot
as novelist of, 132, 135; in *Romola*,
95–97; Spinoza as philosopher of,
33–34; *see* Culture, freedom from nature (artificiality of)

Gambling, 101–2, 106

Haight, Gordon S., 140
Hardy, Barbara, 140
Health, 14, 19–20
Hennell, Caroline. *See* Bray, Cara
Hennell, Charles, 5, 26
Hennell, Rufa (Mrs. Charles, *née* Bra-
bant). *See* Brabant, Rufa
Hennell, Sara, 5, 17

Incarnation, 71, 125, 132, 142n4n5,
145n7; culture as, 30, 56–57; dissociation of ideas from actions and
things, 72, 108–9, 112–17, 122–23;
of ideas in actions and things, 71, 76,
121, 127–31

Languages, 3–4; *see* Syntax
Lewes, Agnes Jervis, finances and, 14;
unfaithfulness of, 10–11
Lewes children (Charles, Thornton, Ber-
tie), at school, 18; Bertie's death, 23;
Thornie's death, 21–22
Lewes George Henry, 6; and George
Eliot: meeting, 9, liaison with,
10–12; death of, 23; occupations, 10;
work of: Goethe biography, 13, essay
on Spinoza, 32, *Problems of Life and
Mind*, 10, 23, *Sea Side Studies*, 13
Lewis, Maria, 2

Mackay, R. W., at *Westminster Review*,
8; *The Progress of the Intellect*, 8,
44–45, 77
Middlemarch, 21, 41, 99, 108–21
The Mill on the Floss, 5–6, 77–89
Money, 14, 16, 19
Multiple plots, in *Daniel Deronda*,
121–31; in *Felix Holt, the Radical*,
103–4, 107; in *Middlemarch*, 110–12;
in *Silas Marner*, 97–100

Narrative voice, 139; and common
ground, 54–55; and community in
The Mill on the Floss, 79–80; as
Feuerbachian species-consciousness,
30; in *Scenes of Clerical Life*, 63,
67–68
Newman, John Henry, 39
Novels, publication format, 17–18

Ordinary life, 54–55; its particularity,
55–56; *see* Concreteness

Parkes, Bessie, 9
Pinney, Thomas, 140
Politics, in *Felix Holt, the Radical*, 105;
in "Mr Gilfil's Love Story," 63–64
Priory, The, 20
Pseudonym, 1, 15–17
Purpose, in *Adam Bede*, 73–74; in *Daniel
Deronda*, 123–25; in *Middlemarch*,
117–18; in *The Mill on the Floss*,
78–79; Spinoza and George Eliot on,
34, 36–37

Reading, 2–3, 7
Reputation, 136–40; problem of sexism
in, 137–38
Resignation, and activity, 58–59, 92,
100; in *The Mill on the Floss*, 83–84;
in *Romola*, 96; instruments of in *Adam
Bede*, 74; *see* Activity
Romola, 18–19, 93–97, 99

Scenes of Clerical Life, 15, 39, 60–68
School, 2–3
Scott, Walter, 3, 135
Secrecy, in *Daniel Deronda*, 122–23,
127–28; in *Felix Holt, the Radical*,
103; in *Middlemarch*, 108–16; in *Ro-
mola*, 95; in *Silas Marner*, 99
Self-betrayal, Arthur Donnithorne,
71–73; Lydgate, 116–17; Tito Me-
lema, 94–95
Sexism. *See* Women
Sibree, John, 7
Silas Marner, 18, 97–102; governing
metaphors in, 97–99
Social estrangement, 11–12, 14

Spanish Gypsy, The, 20–21, 38, 41

Spencer, Herbert, 9–10

Spinoza, 13–14, 32–39, 140; and freedom, 33–34, 38; and George Eliot's life and views, 36–39; as a Jew, 38; on factionalism, 34; on purpose, 34, 36–37

Strauss, David Friedrich, *Das Leben Jesu,* 1835–36 [*The Life of Jesus,* trans. Marian Evans, 1846], 5–6, 25, 26, 142n3

Stump, Reva, 140

Sympathy, 29, 90–93; a definition of, 95; fanaticism of, 113

Syntax, 42, 82

Thale, Jerome, 140

Travel, 11–15, 16, 17, 18, 19, 20, 21, 24

Trust, and confession in *Daniel Deronda,* 127; and individual creativity, 134; for Romola, 100; for Silas Marner, 100; for Tito Melema, 94–95

Westminster Review, 7–10, 13

White, William Hale (pseudonym, Mark Rutherford), 9

Women, analysis of sexist culture in *Daniel Deronda,* 110, 144ch5n4; in *Middlemarch,* 110, 120–21; in *The Mill on the Floss,* 80–83; in *Felix Holt, the Radical,* 104–105; views on, 42–44

DATE DUE

MR 27 '87	MR 26 '87		
GAYLORD			PRINTED IN U.S.A.